AF559737

ATTITUDE TOWARDS SOCIAL STUDIES AND ACHIEVEMENT IN SOCIAL STUDIES

By

Gottipati Satya Narayana

M.A., M.Ed., M.Phil.
Lecturer in Social Studies
Rayapati Venkata Ranga Rao
College of Elementary Education
JKC Road, Guntur – 522006
Andhra Pradesh

Editor

Dr. Digumarti Bhaskara Rao

M.Sc., M.A., M.A., M.Ed., Ph.D.
Reader & Research Director
R.V.R. College of Education
Srinivasa Nagar Colony
Guntur – 522006
digumartibhaskararao@rediffmail.com

D P H

DISCOVERY PUBLISHING HOUSE PVT. LTD.
NEW DELHI-110 002

ISBN: 978-81-8356-261-4

Atrtitude Towards Social Studies and Achievement in Social Studies

Published by:
DISCOVERY PUBLISHING HOUSE
4383/4B, Ansari Road, Darya Ganj
New Delhi-110 002 (India)
Phone: +91-11-23279245; 23253475; 43596065
+91 9811179893 / +91 9871656464
E-mail: discoverybooksindia@gmail.com
orderdphbooks@gmail.com
namitwasan9@gmail.com
web: www.discoverypublishinggroup.com

Printed at:
Infinity Imaging Systems
Delhi

Dedicated
to
Beloved Brother
Dr. K. Subba Rao, Ph.D.
Principal
ASR College of Education
in recognition
of his services
to Teacher Education

PREFACE

Social Studies is the field of study that deals with man and his relations with other people and his environment. Its content is drawn from several Social Sciences and bears a direct relationship with the purposes for which it is taught in schools. Broadly speaking, these purposes include an understanding of human relations, knowledge of the environment, dedication to the basic principles and values of the society, and a commitment to participation in the processes through which that society is maintained and improved. One of the primary concerns of Social Studies, therefore, is to promote an understanding of man's way of living, his basic needs, the activities in which he engages to meet his needs—social, economic, culture and political—and the institutions he has developed with his knowledge and initiation.

Understanding the importance of Social Studies at secondary school level, a study has been undertaken to study the attitude of secondary school students' towards Social Studies and achievement of secondary school students in Social Studies. The secondary school students are holding high attitude towards Social Studies and the gender, locality of the school, management of the school and medium of instruction have no influence on the attitude towards Social Studies possessed by the students. The secondary school students are possessing high achievement in Social Studies and gender and locality of the school are not having influence on the achievement in Social Studies, but management of the school and medium if instruction have their influence on the achievement in Social Studies. There is no significant association between attitude towards Social Studies and achievement in Social Studies of secondary school students and there is no influence of gender and management and there is influence of locality of the school and medium of instruction on the attitude towards Social Studies and achievement in Social Studies. The parents, teachers and students should collectively work for the retainment of the high attitude towards Social Studies and high achievement in Social Studies in order to excel in every walk of life in future and to become useful citizen of India.

Dr. D. Bhaskara Rao

Sri Sai Soudha
D-43, S.V.N. Colony
Guntur 522006
A.P., India

CONTENTS

1

INTRODUCTION

One of the national goals of our country is the establishment of a vital democracy through the development of enlightened and responsible citizenry imbibed with an abiding faith in democratic principles, processes and values. The school has to play an important role in the achievement of this goal, and a large share of that responsibility is to be shouldered by the subject referred to as Social Studies.

Social Studies is the field of study which deals with man and his relations with other people and his environment. Its content is drawn from several Social Sciences and bears a direct relationship with the purposes for which it is taught in schools. Broadly speaking, these purposes include an understanding of human relations, knowledge of the environment, dedication to the basic principles and values of the society, and a commitment to participation in the processes through which that society is maintained and improved in its quality in every perspective. One of the primary concerns of Social Studies, therefore, is to promote an understanding of man's way of living, his basic needs, the activities in which he engages to meet his needs—social, economic, culture and political—and the institutions he has developed with his knowledge and initiation with all pervading quality in every aspect concerned.

Social Studies keeps before itself the educational purpose of developing a rational and scientific approach to social problems and issues that come across in every walk of life. This can be fulfilled only by fostering in the learners the ability to discern the point at an issue to shift from the relevant to irrelevant to marshal ideas in a logical sequence and to express themselves with effective lucidity and perfect effectiveness.

The overall objective of Social Studies, therefore, would be, then, the development of a well-informed and intelligent person, who is alive to current problems and is keen to accept responsibilities as an enlightened citizen. For the welfare of all, he understands the concepts that describe and explain the human society that are so desirable in a democratic society.

Social Studies Education in India

Though Social Studies found its place in the school curriculum in 1937, its content was a part of education in India since the Vedic period. A good part of the curriculum since Vedic period was devoted to the regulation of social behaviour, ethics, need for morals in social life, etc. The history of Social Studies in India could be divided into 5 periods in India, viz., Vedic Period, Post-Vedic Period, Muslim Period, British Period and Post-Independence Period.

The Vedic Period: This period covers the period of Vedas, Upanishads and other great Indian epics. Philosophical orientation was the purpose of education during this time. The emancipation of the soul was looked as the ultimate aim of education. Students were thought the necessity of keeping the mundane pleasures away from life. Religion was considered as the only way to achieve this. Thus, the education was religious. As Mukherjee rightly commented: "Learning in India through the ages had been prized and pursued not for its own sake... but for the sake and as a part of religion". Mukthi or Emancipation was the goal. According to Rawat: Chitta-Vritti-Nirodha" or control of mental activities was connected with the so-called concrete world". Besides Mukthi, Emancipation and Religious Philosophy and some other important aspects were also found their place in the curriculum of Vedic period. Some of them are: 1. Development of the personality of the student. 2. Training in the skills of citizenship and social life.

3. Importing technical and craft education. 4. Inculcating the idea of simple living and high thinking. 5. Development of simple living and high thinking. 6. Education on nature and environment.

The Post-Vedic Period: This period starts from the Buddhism and with the invasion and settlement of Muslim rulers in India. Buddhism and Jainism, the two contemporary and most important religions of India and their education systems, aimed at Nirvana (salvation). Religious discourse was the central to the curriculum though other subjects like logic, accountancy, philosophy, etc., were also taught. Like Buddhist education, the ultimate aim of Jainist education was also salvation. Besides salvation, its purposes included importing right knowledge, right philosophy and right character necessary for the all-round development of an individual.

The Muslim Period: The Muslims conquered India and established their empire in eighteenth century. They introduced a new system of education. The aims of their education were: 1. Propagation of Islam; 2. Islamic social morals; 3. Material progress; and 4. Political support. There was no Government structure to overlook the education. Throughout the Muslim period, educational institutions were maintained with the help of philanthropist donations. Teachers enjoyed complete freedom and prepared syllabus, educational schemes, etc., of their own and implemented them with all freedom. According to Ahmad, the Islamic education was divided into three stages—Primary, Secondary and Higher. The aim of primary education was to teach the pupil the knowledge of the alphabet and religious prayers. The aim of the secondary stage was to teach the Persian grammar and literature. Higher education consisted of logic, philosophy, law, astrology, arithmetic, history, geography, medicine, agriculture, etc., besides grammar and literature.

The British Period: The roots of the modern Indian education were sown by the British. Though the purpose of the education was entirely different, the structure, the stages, structural arrangements, etc., were the contribution of the British in modern India. Unlike the Muslims, who conquered and made India their home, the British conquered India only to exploit its natural resources, but not settle in India and do some favours to this great nation. So, naturally their interest was not in the development of India. They used every institution to exploit India, and education has no exemption. Moreover, the manpower available in Great Britain was not sufficient to control a vast country like India. So, they wanted to use the services in military and in administration of the Indians to control India suitably. The ultimate result was introducing such type of educational system which will ensure a committed pro-British elite educated group of Indians. This was made crystal-clear in the following communiqué by Lord Macaulay, the chief architect of Indian education system; "We must, at present, do our best to form a class who may be interpreters between us and the millions we govern, a class of persons, Indian in blood and colour, but English in taste, in opinion, in morals, and in intellect. And that the great object of the British Government ought to be the promotion of European literature and Science among the natives of India, and that all the funds appropriated for the purpose of education would be employed on English education alone." Initially, the British did not show much interest in education of India. Much of their time was preoccupied with wars and business. As Deva Raj Dutt rightly observed: "The British were neither involved in Indian education nor did they have any clear-cut policy. They were busy in consolidating their political power in the interest of their mother country." Later, the British government also started involving itself in education and its organization, but it was a policy of downward filtration (education of few or only elite) instead of education for everyone. The reason was obvious—it did not want to educate all Indians and it wanted to educate only a few who will act as buffer. At the levels of Primary, Secondary and Higher education, the British wanted to copy the system of education that was prevailing in Britain. The syllabus, examination, evaluation, etc., were the simple replicas of the British system of education.

The Post-Independent Period: India became independent on August 15, 1947. Thus, it got an opportunity to use a system of education for its own development. It set the goal of universal free and compulsory education. It realized that universalization of education is the only alternative to raise its potential in industry and agriculture. But, unfortunately, there was not much change in the system of education, except that Whites were replaced by the Browns in the office. The academicians working in this area are of the opinion that a complete and thorough re-orientation of the entire attitude towards education is necessary to achieve the goals that are set by the fathers of the Indian constitution. By and large, Social Studies seek to foster the objectives, that a general education programme attempts to attain and, therefore, it is to be regarded as an indispensable part of general education at school level.

Meaning of Social Studies

Social Studies is the offspring of Social Sciences that is primarily concerned with the social aspects of human behaviour. The very name itself describes the meaning of the field 'social' meaning concerning the society, and 'studies' implies areas to be learned. Hence, Social Studies is an area that is to be learned about society and its concerns.

The National Council of Educational Research and Training (NCERT) gave the meaning of Social Studies as "A field of study which deals with man, his relations with other men and his environment ... An understanding of human relationships, knowledge of the environment, dedication to the basic principles and values of the society in which it is taught and a commitment to participate in the processes through which that society is maintained and improved." National Council for the Social Studies defined that "Social Studies is an integrated study of the Social Sciences and humanities to promote civic competence".

Wesley and Wronski opined that "Social Studies indicates materials whose contents are predominantly social. The Social Studies utilizes substantive and procedural aspects of the Social Sciences for pedagogical purpose." James High stated that "Most simply stated the Social Studies is the school mirror of the scholarly findings of the Social Sciences.".

"The Social Studies is, as the name suggests, studies of the society and its chief aim is to help pupils to understand the world in which they have to live and how it came to be, so that they may become responsible citizens. It aims at promoting critical thinking, encourages a readiness for social change, an appreciation of other cultures and a realization of other cultures and a realization of the interdependence of man and man and of nation and nation." (J.F. Forrester)

The above definitions reveal that the contents, methods and organization of Social Studies are derived directly from purposes for which they are taught that include an understanding of human relationship, knowledge of the environment, dedication to the basic principles and values of the society, and a commitment to the processes through which the society is maintained and improved. The above constitute what may be called Social Studies.

Thus, Social Studies touches all aspects of human life. It derives from the Social Sciences a body of content focused upon the activities that man undertakes as he meets his fundamental needs. One of the primary concerns of Social Studies is to promote an understanding of man's way of living, his basic needs and the activities in which he engages to meet his needs—social, economic, cultural, and political—and the institution he has developed for his own survival successfully. Therefore, Social Studies is a study of the society in general and the community in particular.

Nature of Social Studies

There is a question on the nature of Social Studies, whether it is a Science or an Art? Many scholars were hesitant to place that in any one of these two compartments and consider Social Studies as both a Science and an Art.

If the broader meaning of the word 'Science' is considered, Social Studies can be broadly called Science, when Science is defined as a body of systematized knowledge, and its function is to establish a relationship between cause and effect and deduce generalizations. In the words of Garner, "Science is a knowledge relating to a particular subject acquired by a systematic observation, experience or study which has been coordinated, systematized and classified." Science, thus, is a collection of facts of a particular type. The facts are classified and systematized on the basis of their degree of accuracy. Conveniently, Science can be classified into three groups: viz., abstract science, natural science and social science. Abstract sciences are concerned to Logic and

Philosophy. Natural Sciences include both Physical Sciences which deal with physical phenomena such as Physics, Chemistry, Geology and Astronomy, and the Biological Sciences, such as Botany and Zoology. Social Sciences include all those sciences which study social life in its various forms as it is done in case of observation, experiment, analysis, etc., although its laws are not so exact and definite like in natural science. Therefore, in this sense, Social Studies is a Science. But, classification of facts and the formulation of laws that are mutually consistent and universally valid upon the basis of rational judgments constitute the essential aim of modern Science. But social phenomena are perpetually undergo change and are difficult to control. Social Studies, it must be admitted, can not be an exact Science.

Social Studies is considered as an Art as it is defined as "human skill as opposed to nature". However, Art, in its broader sense, also implies the practical application of Science to get knowledge about social life and institutions simply for the sake of knowledge, and its purpose is to create an active and intelligent interest among the citizens to secure a better life. Hence, Social Studies can be considered as an art of living as a good citizen.

We can say that Social Studies is both a Science and an Art in the sense that it investigates conditions and seeks to apply the results of its investigations to the furtherance of human welfare.

Branches of Social Studies

Social Studies represents a broad and composite institutional area that deals with a variety of needs and problems of man so as to make the child acquaint with his past and present geographical and social environment. It draws the information from different Social Sciences such as History, Geography, Civics and Economics in order to unfold gradually the total environment of the child with reference to physical, social and cultural elements. History, Geography, Civics and Economics are to be taught in Social Studies so that the vital elements are fused in a way, which are relevant for entertaining and amplifying children's day-to-day economic, social and civic experiences, and to develop an insight into effective human relationships, good social values and right personal attitudes.

Each branch has its own contribution to the teaching of Social Studies. 1. History makes an attempt to answer the questions how our present life has come in to being and what was the quality of inheritance of which we are the heirs. It gives the youth an insight, appreciation and understanding of historical and cultural perspectives and problems. 2. Geography trains the future citizens to imagine accurately the conditions of the stage of the great world so that they may think sensibly about political and social and practical problems in the world. 3. Civics provides realistic and first-hand knowledge and experience leading to the improvement of daily living in home, school and community and the eventual participation by pupils in the life of the country in a democratic manner. 4. Economics makes the child familiar with the multifarious economic activities of life and the economic structure of the society that would help him to meet his basic needs and offer him various channels of vocations and professions at the close of his school career. It is to help the child know the natural resources of his country and how he can make maximum use of them to improve conditions of living, the necessary complementary between production and consumption, and how human goals can be achieved through effective planning.

Social Studies and Social Sciences

Social Studies is a field that studies human relationships. But, often the term Social Studies has been treated as a synonym to Social Sciences, yet, there is a considerable difference between the two. Despite the fact that both Social Studies and Social Sciences deal with human relationship, they differ in their scope. Moreover, they differ in their standards and purposes too. Generally speaking, Social Sciences concentrates on investigation, research and solution to social problems; whereas Social Studies is more or less is a descriptive type when the information is truly presented.

The Social Sciences is concerned with the areas of knowledge dealing with the relationships of human beings with each other and with their natural environment called the society. They include such areas as history, economics, political science, anthropology, sociology, geography, etc. The Social Sciences presents the story of human affairs from the past to our contemporary life and the

Social Studies may be considered in terms of knowledge drawn from the Social Sciences and contemporary life for instructional purposes in aiding the youth in becoming good citizens.

Thus, the Social Studies, as a field of enquiry, aids students through sound knowledge, information and the functional experiences which are essential to the building of basic values, desirable habits and accepted attitudes and worthwhile skills basic to effective citizenship; whereas the subject matter of Social Sciences can be used in understanding trends, solving problems and revealing the past as a means towards better understanding of the present. Understanding of the Social Sciences gives a broader knowledge and a complete picture of the growth of modern civilization. In fact, today's civilization with all its complexities needs the fruits of the Social Sciences for better understanding, and the fundamental test of the Social Sciences is accuracy, reliability and eventual test of the Social Studies is instructional utility. Though, the Social Studies is also under obligations to be accurate and reliable, it automatically meets this requirement by including faithful portions or versions of Social Sciences.

Generally, the term Social Sciences is applied to the research materials about human beings and their interrelationships. A report on political parties, a monograph on business cycles, and an analysis of budget and its affect on the state economy, etc., are some of the examples of materials that belong to the Social Sciences which are concerned with the detailed, systematic and logical study of human relationships.

In contrast, the Social Studies is designed primarily for instructional purposes. They are those portions or aspects of Social Sciences that have been selected and adopted for use in the school or in other instructional situations. The Social Studies is Social Sciences, but simplified for pedagogical purposes and consists of materials of instruction. Hence, we can say that Social Sciences represents an adult-centred approach, while the Social Studies represents a child-centered approach.

From the above discussion, it can be said that the Social Studies summarizes what has already been ascertained in Social Sciences. Hence, the primary purpose of this field is to disseminate information. So, it has no contemporary reference. On the other hand, Social Sciences has social applications and are contemporary. It understands the present conditions and problems and recognizes the ultimate social purposes of the people. Hence Social Sciences is useful not only to present generations, but also beneficial to the future generations.

The focus and emphasis of both are different. For example, when a student studies Geography as a Social Science, he has to focus his attention on the methods of Geography, the tools and concepts of the subject and knowledge which will provide a basis for future specialization at a later stage. The student studying Geography as part of Social Studies, the programmes should focus attention on using ideas and concepts from Geography to understand man and various parts of the world and how geographical factors influence the relationship between groups of men and nation today.

Moreover, Social Studies and Social Science differ in their scope. The Social Sciences is far larger than Social Studies. Social Sciences observes, verifies, measures and quantifies the phenomenon. The basic purpose of any Social Sciences is to discover universal and everlasting truths. Social Studies do not indulge in any exercise that involves observation and verification. It does not probe into any social event. Social Studies simply presents a phenomenon as it was accepted by the majority. Questions like 'why', 'how' and 'when' are kept beyond the scope of Social Studies, whereas Social Sciences starts with 'why'.

Furthermore, both differ in their aim also. The primary aim of Social Studies is instructional utility where studies are primarily meant to the formal groups, but Social Sciences is interested in the society at large.

To conclude, there is no hard and past line separating Social Sciences and Social Studies. At the primary classes, where gradual enfoldment of the total environment—physical, social and cultural—is needed, Social Studies is to be taught. As the student becomes a competent investigator and interpreter of raw data in the middle and secondary stages, he emerges from the Social Studies into the Social Sciences.

Aims and Objectives of Social Studies

The main ides in setting up of aims and objectives is to make the teacher aware of the values to be attained so that they are able to plan teaching programme to select significant and meaningful content to choose suitable teaching methods and techniques and to use appropriate devices for teaching. True, the aims may be idealist, remote and difficult, but they are not useless. In this connection, Wesley has rightly remarked that "the star is useful though the mariner never reaching". Infact, aims are a true compass to make our journey in the pedagogical sea safe and secure. Speaking more elaborately, they help us in knowing the scope of the subject and the standard of that grade. In short, they are the crux and key of the entire process of teaching and learning.

So as to obey the general aims and objectives of education, every subject and activity in the school should contribute to those aims and objectives. So, naturally, the aims and objectives of Social Studies will have to be in consonance with the broader aims of education here and now. In this connection, John V. Michalls has rightly remarked that "the centre of Social Studies is identical with those of general aims and objectives of education".

The Education Commission (1964-66), which was appointed by the Government of India to advise the government on the national pattern of education and on the general principles and policies of the development of education at all stages and in all aspects, stated that "The aim of teaching Social Studies is to help the students to acquire knowledge of their environment and values which are vital for intelligent participation in the affairs of the community, the state, the nation and the world". Besides this, some other aims and objectives are identified as: 1. To acquaint the child with his past and present geographical and social environment; 2. To enable children to appreciate India's rich cultural heritage; 3. To enable to recognize and get rid of what is undesirable and antiquated, especially in the context of social change; 4. To build social competence; 5. To build intelligent democratic citizenship; 6. To help the child acquire the right attitudes, knowledge, understanding and competence which we will need in the interaction with social and physical environment; 7. To help the child gain insights into spiritual, economic and political valuable forces in human behaviour and human relationships; 8. To provide a pattern and experience of study that will serve as a foundation for later specializations; 9. To develop desirable qualities for an all-round development of a rich personality; 10. To enable the pupils to use their leisure properly; 11. To interpret the past as a background for improving the future; 12. To foster national feelings.

The above discussion thus has been concerned chiefly with the general aims of Social Studies. But along with those general aims there are specific aims for each grade or class which is in consonance with the broad aims of Social Studies at each grade. Broadly, the schooling was divided into two stages: viz., primary school stage and secondary school stage. Let us see the aims of teaching Social Studies at each level.

I. Specific Aims of Teaching Social Studies at Primary Level

1. To help the child to explore and understand his social and cultural environment; 2. To develop in the child a sense of belongingness towards the society through gradual widening of his mental horizon from his home and school to the wide world; 3. To acquaint the child with the world of work and to develop in him respect for human labour; 4. To encourage the child to understand that we are striving to build a better life for all; 5. To impress on the child's mind, as he grows, that ours is a rich and composite culture in the formation of which people of different faiths, religions and linguistic groups have made valuable contribution; 6. To develop among children respect for all religions and their places and ways of worship; 7. To encourage the child to understand that we all are equal irrespective of sex, creed, language, etc., and that these are no superior or inferior people and that we all co-operate and organize ourselves to solve our problems; 8. To impress on the child that India, in keeping with the cultural heritage, is one of the important countries of the world that is active in promoting peace, understanding and co-operation among the nations of the world.

II. *Specific Aims of Teaching Social Studies at Secondary Level*

In the secondary stage, the field of Social Studies consists of various subjects like Geography, History, Civics and Economics, so as to provide a background for understanding the present trends. The specific aims of each subjects should be in harmony with the broader aims of each subject should be in harmony with the broader aims of Social Studies. Let us see the specific aims of each subject.

History: 1. To promote an understanding of the common roots of human civilization and an appreciation of the basic unity of mankind; 2. To develop an appreciation of the contribution made by various cultures to the total heritage of mankind; 3. To foster the understanding that the mutual interaction of various cultures has been an important factor in the progress of mankind; 4. To facilitate the study of the history of specific countries in relation to and as part of the general history of mankind.

Geography: 1. To gain an understanding of man and his environment; 2. To help students identify the varieties in the distribution of physical and economical phenomena over the surface of the earth, that are associated and give a distinctive character to particular parts of the earth's surface; 3. To help students analyze the ways of life of the people all over the world, their problems in the light of their varying environments and their status of economic and technical development; 4. To develop an appreciation of interdependence of various geographical regions; 5. To help students make generalization with the help of geographical concepts, the knowledge of which is of great value in understanding, evaluating and reaching decisions about world problems.

Civics: 1. To promote active and intelligent citizens who have the necessary civic competence to participate in the community affairs effectively; 2. To develop an intelligent understanding of the structure and working of the civic and political institutions of India; 3. To help the students appreciate the role of the United Nations and Indian's contribution towards maintenance of world peace; 4. To respect each person with regard to his race, colour, creed or sex.

Economics: 1. To appreciate the importance of economic systems; 2. To understand the causes of inflation and deflation gap; 3. To train the students in economic citizenship; 4. To aid the students in acquiring a knowledge and understanding of the fundamental principles of our economic life; 5. To understand the inter-relationship between the economic principles and the problems that are confronted in our day-to-day life.

III. *Specific Objectives of Social Studies*

In order to accomplish the said aims, certain specific objectives need to be set up and achieved.

The specific objectives of Social Studies can be said as understanding, acquiring knowledge, develop right type of attitudes, formation of habits and skills. The basic purpose of Social Studies programme is to provide the motivation, understanding, knowledge and skills necessary for informed and active citizenship. Ideally, each pupil who completes the programme should be motivated to support these principles actively as a patriotic and participating citizen.

The selection of Social Studies materials for inclusion in the school curriculum is intended to offer opportunities for each pupil to develop: 1. Knowledge and understanding of how various groups of people have developed social institutions suited to their needs and how various people have encountered the problems in developing their respective cultures and civilizations; 2. Knowledge and understanding of the historical backgrounds of the government and institutions developed by the people and of the social, economic and political problems faced by a country and its people; 3. Understanding of and a loyalty to the principles upon which the government is based; 4. Understanding of the problems faced by the people in a democratic country; 5. Certain skills, habits and attitudes are essential to good citizenship in a democratic country; those include the personal skills needed by each individual to make use of the varied sources of information commonly available in the field of Social Sciences; 6. In addition, skills and attitudes are included which are requisite to life in a society in which each citizen is expected to work co-operatively with others and to assume proper obligation of citizenship.

With the above points of information, any one can feel that the subject Social Studies is one of the important subjects of learning at secondary school level.

Attitude Towards Social Studies

The concept of attitudes is an old one in psychology, and we tend to associate it more directly with the area of social psychology. It was first used in America by Franklin H. Giddings, the sociologist, and was introduced in to social psychology by William I. Thomas. The first American psychologist to use the concept in a general text book was Howard C. Warren in his 'Human Psychology'.

Allport referred attitude to as the most distinctive and indispensable concept in contemporary American social psychology. Thurston boldly asserted that attitude can be measured. The concept of attitudes, no doubt, gained more general acceptance by American psychologists as a result of the influence of Giddings and Thomas, both of whom were professional sociologists.

The concept of attitude has several characteristics that differentiate it from other concepts referring to internal states of the individual. Sherif and Sherif (1968) state that: 1. Attitudes are innate, they belong to that domain of human motivation variously studied under the labels of social drives, social needs, social orientation and the like. It is assumed that the appearance of an attitude is dependent on learning; 2. Attitudes are not temporary states but are more or less enduring once they are formed. Of course, attitudes do change, but formed, they acquire regulatory function such that, within limits, they are not subject to change with the ups and downs of homeostatic functioning of the organism or with every first-noticeable variation in stimulus conditions; 3. Attitudes always imply a relationship between the person and objects. In other words, attitudes are not self-generated psychologically. They are formed or learned in relation to identifiable referents, whether these be persons, groups, institutions, objects, values, social issues or ideologies; 4. The relationship between person and object is not neutral but has motivational affective properties. These properties derive from the context of highly significant social interaction in which many attitudes are formed, from the fact that the objects are not neutral for the participants and from the fact that self, as it develops, acquires positive value for the person. Therefore, the self, as it develops, acquires positive value for the person. Therefore, the linkage between self and social environment is seldom neutral; 5. The subject-object relationship is accomplished through the formation of categories both differentiating between the persons positive or negative relation to objects in various categories. The referent of an attitude constitutes a set that may range, theoretically, from one to the large number of objects. However, in actuality, the formation of a positive or negative stand towards one object usually implies differential attachment to other in the same domain.

Aggarwal (1964) summarizes the concept of attitude through these characteristics: 1. There is no limited range of attitudes, our likes and dislikes, food we take and everything is an aspect of attitude; 2. It is a position towards the objects, either for or against; 3. There is individual difference in attitudes; 4. They are the bases of behaviour as they lead to strike, war, voting, etc.; 5. They may be avert or covert; 6. They are integrated into an organized system; 7. They are acquired, but not inborn; 8. Attitude towards an object is not necessarily based on its utility; 9. They differ from culture to culture; 10. They are more or less lasting but they can be modified.

Gordon W. Allport (1967) selected some representative characteristics of attitude, which are: 1. It is readiness for attention or action of a definite sort (Baldwin, 1901-1905); 2. Attitude is literally mental posture, guide for conduct to which each new experience is referred to before responses are made; 3. An attitude is a complex of feelings, desires, convictions, prejudices or other tendencies that have given a set or act to a person because of varied experiences (Chave, 1928); 4. An attitude is a mental disposition of the individual to act for or against a definite object; 5. An attitude denotes the general set of the organism as a whole towards an object or situation which calls for adjustment (Lundberg, 1920); 6. Attitude is a mode of emotional regard for object and motor "set" or slight tentative reaction towards them (Ower, 1929);

7. An attitude is more or less permanently enduring state of readiness of mental organization which predisposes an individual to react in a characteristic way to any object or situation with which it is related.

The importance of attitudes is very great. They permeate our whole life and our self-concept that is essentially the sum total of attitudes by which we live. They make a great difference in almost everyone's life. They offer great possibilities for successful achievement as well as failure in life. Efficiency results when a person is impelled by his attitude to start, continue and complete a project rather than to avoid an unpleasant task.

The attitude of an individual towards his work affects his worthwhileness in the activity. The businessman depends upon the favourable attitude of his customers towards his product and services to keep his business going. The politician must have favourable attitudes towards his personality ability and political behaviour in order to count on his re-election. The hard working person has favourable attitudes towards all those experiences and situations in which hard work is necessary. The successful teacher has favourable attitudes towards his students, his friends, his subjects and his principal. The person who considers himself very clever tries to be clever in all situations.

Attitudes are considered as important motivators of behaviour and affect all human values. Crow and Crow (1973) wrote that "His attitude towards others determines his social values. If the individual can learn to forget self and to be of service to those who need help, he has achieved personality characteristics that are essential to the gaining of appreciation from others. If he does not feel superior to the work that he is doing or to the people with whom he is associated, he is likely to succeed in his work in his social relationship."

There are, indeed, very few acts or decisions in everyday affairs that do not somehow take account of the way in which attitudes may be affected. Therefore, the cultivation of attitude towards these values and ideas which society cherishes and appreciates is the best way of promoting behaviour consistent with the accepted codes and morals of the social order.

From the point of view of learning, attitudes are important in as much as they facilitate further learning and thus contain within themselves the course of further motivation. Attitude must be aroused and developed for a child. Every school cannot escape from their responsibility of organizing a deliberate plan and programme of influencing positive attitudes in the child.

The child should not be permitted to do completely as he wishes. He should be stimulated towards desirable activity through the arousal of interest in worthwhile projects. Constructive and objective attitudes during childhood support well during adolescence. The attitude of the teacher or of the parent or of a group leader is important. Each should display the kind of objective but understanding attitude that will be a good attitude for the child to imitate.

Education of the child, therefore, must include the development of right attitudes as well as the acquisition of good behavioural habits that are socially desirable. Not only some rules and regulations concerning good conduct and effective playing habits be taught, but they should be understood and appreciated in the light of their values to the individual and society.

Promoting favourable attitudes, therefore, in an individual is an asset both to him and to society. Promoting favourable attitude towards social studies education is to encourage him to take part in social studies education programme and still further the individual should be aided in making deliberate choice of behaviour in harmony with his own and society's betterment. He should strive to create favourable attitudes and eliminate unfavourable ones.

To use the concept of attitudes in understanding and predicting action, one needs reliable and valid measurement. The measurement of attitudes like the measurement of all psychological determinants is necessarily indirect. Attitude can be measured only on the basis of inference drawn from the responses of the individual towards the object, his overt actions and his verbal statements of the beliefs, feelings and dispositions to act with respect to the object. The beliefs, feelings and dispositions to act with respect to Social Studies, it would be referred to as attitude towards Social Studies.

Considering the very role of attitude towards Social Studies at secondary school level, this study is intending to study the level of attitude possessed by the secondary school students towards Social Studies.

Attitude Towards Social Studies and Achievement in Social Studies

The attitudes of individuals have been always influencing the achievement of individuals in different dimensions of life and career. Knowing pretty well the importance of this phenomenon, this study intends to study the association between attitude towards Social Studies and achievement in Social Studies.

STATEMENT OF THE PROBLEM

"A Study of Attitude towards Social Studies and Achievement in Social Studies of Secondary School Students".

NEED OF THE STUDY

This study helps in identifying the attitude of secondary school students towards Social Studies and their achievement in Social Studies; both are to be known necessary as Social Studies is one of the compulsory subjects of school education.

The levels of attitude and achievement will help the teachers and administrators along with the students and parents in enhancing their status. Hence, this study has been undertaken for a detailed study of identifying their levels and their interrelationship.

OBJECTIVES OF THE STUDY

The following objectives are framed for the present study:

1. To find out the level of attitude towards Social Studies and achievement in Social Studies of secondary school students;
2. To compare the level of attitude towards Social Studies and achievement in Social Studies between boys and girls, rural and urban students, English medium and Telugu medium students and private and government secondary school students;

3. To find out the association between attitude towards Social Studies and achievement in Social Studies of secondary school students;

4. To compare the association between attitude towards Social Studies and achievement in Social Studies of boys and girls rural and urban students, English medium and Telugu medium students and private and government secondary school students.

SCOPE OF THE STUDY

Social Studies is one of the compulsory subjects at secondary school level. It prepares good citizens besides fulfilling many aims and objectives of education. Considering the very role of Social Studies education in human living, the present study is limited to the study of attitude towards Social Studies and achievement in Social Studies of secondary school students. Consideration was given to variables such as gender of the student, locality of school, type of management and medium of instruction. This study is confined to 10th class students studying the secondary schools of Guntur district.

2

REVIEW OF RELATED LITERATURE

Any worthwhile research study in any field of knowledge requires an adequate familiarity with the work which has already been done in the same area. A summary of the writings of recognized authorities and of previous research provides evidence that the research is familiar with what is already known and what is still unknown and untested. Since effective research is based upon past knowledge, this step helps to eliminate the duplication of what has been already done. It is a valuable guide to define the problem, to recognize its significance, to suggest promising data gathering devices, to appropriate study design, to identify sources of data, to make effective analysis and to arrive at fruitful conclusions.

Citing studies that show substantial agreement and those that seem to present conflicting conclusions helps to sharpen and define understanding of existing knowledge in the problem a long list of annotated studies relating to the problem is ineffective and inappropriate. Only those studies that are plainly relevant, competently executed, and clearly reported should be considered.

Educational opportunities, through open to all, do not seem to engage to any reasonable extent the capacities of those who seek to avail themselves of them. An eternal question baffling parents, educators and planers is: why do students of demonstrated ability flop in their academic efforts at school or college examination?

Academic underachievement, more than academic failure, constitutes a grave problem as it amounts to wastage of human resources which is construed as an irreparable loss to the society, which a developing country like India can ill-afford. This stimulated a number of researchers to undertake studies, like the present study, on factors influencing achievement; a review of which is presented hereunder.

There are a number of researches on achievement and the factors that are influencing the achievement of students. Achievement is influenced by many factors like values, intelligence, creativity, socio-economic status, the level of aspiration. Some of the important findings of various researchers on different factors are cited hereunder.

Taylor (1964) stated that the value, the student places upon his own worth, effects his academic achievement. Very low level of expectation tends to make a pupil accept very low standard of achievement, very high expectation leads to discouragement and diminished effort because he feels he cannot live up to what is required of him. To be practical, the level of expectation needs to be general to suit to each individual's capability.

Acharyulu (1978,) while studying interactive effects of creativity on achievement, found that intelligence has positive effect on academic achievement. Menon (1980) has also found the same results. This was in agreement with the result of Vijayalakshimi (1980).

The study of Singh (1982) again showed that verbal, non-verbal and total creative thinking variables had positive and significant relationship with academic achievement of high school boys and girls.

Mukharji (1970) found that intelligence had significantly positive influence on scholastic achievement.

Zacharia (1977) attempted to find out the effect of attitude and interest on the achievement in Social Studies of pupils of tenth grade. He found that there was a positive correlation between the secondary school pupil's achievement in Social Studies and their attitude. The pupil's interest in Social Studies was closely related to their achievement in the subject at all levels.

Zacharia (1977) found that the pupil's intelligence was a major factor in influencing their achievement in Social Studies and observed that pupils attitude and intelligence scores were more or less equally correlated with their achievement in Social Studies. But pupil's intelligence was not a prominent factor in influencing their attitude and interest in Social Studies.

George (1966) revealed that the pupils with high intelligence and higher achievers had better adjustment in all the groups studied.

Reddy (1978) found that adjustment has significantly related to scholastic performance. Among other results, it is of significance to note that the attitude to self, learning, achievement, parents, teachers and peers were found to be positively academic adjustment and scholastic performance.

Soman (1977) investigated the overlapping of fourteen affective variables belonging to basic personality's dimension of achievement in mathematics. This revealed that personal adjustment variables and anxiety variables had a considerable influence on achievement in mathematics. The dominant personality factor identified for the over achievers was individual adjustment factor.

Students' home, health, social and emotional adjustment, students' study habits and their attitude towards education figured as some of the non-intellectual correlates of academic achievement in a study by Chopra (1988). The study showed that academic achievement has positive relationship with attitude towards education and also with the study habits of students. Further, home adjustment was found to be more closely related to academic than emotional, health and social adjustment.

Pyari (1980) found that the relationship between family attachment scores and educational achievement scores was found to be negatively significant. Theoretical, aesthetic, social and religious values were positively and significantly related with educational achievement, while economic and political values were negatively and significantly related.

Satyanandam (1969) highlighted two sub-aspects of socio-economic status, namely, educational level of parents and economic status of parents. According to the researcher, the children of graduate parents performed far better than the children of matriculate parents. Children of upper and lower and upper and middle economic strata only differed significantly on the variable of academic affairs.

Chatterji, et al. (1971) investigated the effect of parent's education, family size and general condition of the home upon scholastic achievement. They found that the economic conditions of the family have no effect upon the scholastic achievement in all the intellectual ability groups. Similarly, possession of a study room had no favourable effect in increasing the achievement score in almost all the cases. The family size and the number of siblings were inversely related to the scholastic achievement especially in the low intellectual level. Parents' help has significant positive contribution towards higher achievement; and parents' educational level was directly related to the achievement of their children. But father's occupation did not show considerable effect. However, the study conclusively demonstrated parent's education has related to scholastic achievement. This argument was strengthened by the study of Khanna (1980) by establishing a significant and positive relationship between socio-economic status and academic achievement. But socio-economic status was found unrelated to academic achievement in the study of Salunke (1979) even though he found that educational facilities and emotional happiness in home contributed positively to the pupils' performance.

Siddiqui (1979), while studying the effect of achievement motivation and personality on academic achievement, found that there was a mutual relationship between intelligence, achievement and personality; and personality has a positive correlation with achievement motivation.

Singh and Kumar (1977) and Bushan and Ahuja (1977), while inquiring in to the relationship of anxiety and achievement, came to the conclusion that anxiety has a negative relationship with achievement. But contrary to this, Ravindar (1977) revealed that general anxiety by itself had little effect on academic achievement and that combination of anxiety with intelligence considerably increased the accuracy of predicting academic performance. Yet, in another study, Hussain (1977) gave the conclusion that anxiety was found to bear a curvilinear relationship with academic achievement.

Shah (1978) studied self-concept as a major variable and looked into its relationship with achievement. He has given the conclusion that the relationship between self-concept and academic achievement was significantly positive and linear. In agreement with this conclusion, Goswamy (1978) added that the rural students tended to have a good self-concept than the urban ones.

Jain (1978) found that bright achievers were characterized by better study habits and higher achievement motivation than dull achievers.

Agarwal (1975), who made psycho-social study of academic under-achievement, concluded that under-achievers were comparatively less emotionally mature, less calm, less placed, less prone to getting in to difficulties, less able to face reality, and possessing less ego strength than over-achievers. On comparison, over-achievers had stronger educational, social and humanistic values than under-achievers.

The studies, concluded by Nagpal (1979), Saun (1980), and Patel and Joshi (1977) revealed that the under-achievers have social, adjustment, emotional, etc., problems in comparison to over-achievers. In Nagpal's study, the under-achievers reported a greater number of adjustment problems and more academic adjustment problems. Same conclusions were drawn from the study of Saun. The high-achievers were well adjusted with family and were also better adjustment personality than the under-achievers. A variety of conclusions were drawn in the study of Ghuman (1976). It showed that over-achievers and under-achievers did not differ significantly on the variables, namely, attitudes, achievement motivation or personality traits. The study attributed over-achievement primarily to non-intellective personality variables and under-achievement to intellective factors.

Taking into consideration the climate in the institution as one of the variables in the study and working on a sample of scheduled caste students, Rani (1980) and Shashidhar (1981) concluded that academic achievement was influenced, among other things, by institutional factors. Desai (1979) and Hirunval (1980) found a positive relationship between class room climate and pupils' academic achievement. Furthermore, an increase in school conditions was likely to lead to better achievement. (Subramanyam, 1981). In, yet, another study Srinivasarao and Subramanyam (1982) reported similar results.

Menon (1972) found that job aspiration, educational aspiration and general ambition were strongly associated with high achievement, particularly in girls. Ram Kumar (1972) observed a strong association between achievement and goal discrepancy. Agreeing with these results, Kuppuswami (1974) observed that the achievement in school was closely related to the level of aspiration.

In contrary, studies of Gould and Koplan (1940), Sears (1940), Holt (1942), Schultz and Recciuti (1954) found no relationship between scholastic achievement and level of aspiration. Sharma (1979) also found that the level of aspiration did not influence academic achievement. But the studies of Shukla (1973) revealed that the level of aspiration determines the limits of academic achievement to some extent only.

Godgil made an investigation into the causes of failures in Social Sciences in the public examination at the end of standard 10th by the S.S.C.E Board, Pune, in March 1968. The main conclusions drawn from the study were: failures in Social Sciences were due to the inadequacies is grading the subject, in mastering the subject by teachers, in guidance in writing answers, and unsatisfactory translations of the question papers from English into other languages. Another factor is poor equipment in the schools, which creeps into the results. Another reason he found out for large scale failures was due to lack of required percentage of qualified teachers to teach Social Sciences.

Achievement in Social Studies was not hindered because of medium of instruction (Mishra, et al., 1973). But, it was not in conformity with the results of Anand (1973).

Pandey (1974) found that achievement in Social Studies has an effect with the background from which the students come. The industrial background was more favourable for high academic achievement than rural background. But in the study of Patel (1977), it was observed that there was no significant difference in achievement between urban boys and urban girls; but in case of rural areas, girls were superior to boys, and he added, that there is a direct relationship between achievement in History and Geography and age.

A study by Fernandaz, Massey, and Dornburch (1976) revealed that the Social Studies enjoys esteem among students, that yet the best could be described as modest. Students were found to believe that competence in their Social Studies was much less important for success in their future occupational roles than competence in their other subjects. This view was reinforced by similar beliefs on the part of parents, counselors and friends. The investigators noted that because students viewed Social Studies classes as unimportant, they were unwilling to expand a great deal of effort on their students in this area. Further, there was a widespread belief among students that if they did 'poor work' in their Social Studies classes they still would receive an acceptable high grade. The investigators concluded that the students' tendencies to view Social Studies instruction as unimportant and academically soft were rooted in students' lack of specific understanding of the knowledge and skills central to the Social Studies, and in students' failure to see any personal benefit deriving from lessons in Social Studies.

The above findings show that the problems of achievement, especially in Social Studies, attracted considerable attention and that there were so many angels to study this problem. The topic still considered to be important from the point of social utility as a very large number of students were showing under-achievement in their Social Studies, even in case of top scorers when the whole examination was considered as their academic achievement. Hence, this study has been taken up for study.

3

DESIGN OF THE STUDY

Research design is a framework for every research problem. Research design is the plan and the strategy of investigation conceived so as to obtain answers to the research questions (Kerlinger). It is a process of deliberate anticipation dedicated towards bringing out an unexpected situation under control.

Designing is regarded as the heart of the study, because it is that part of the study which decides the fate of the research. It is upon the design that the nature of data to be collected will very much depends and it helps in collecting and analyzing data in an economic, efficient and relevant manner. Therefore, it is desirable to have a methodologically well designed research plan.

In the present chapter, the following four aspects that are concerned with the design of the present study have been discussed.

The research procedure includes the operational definitions of the different terms used in the study, the geographical area, hypotheses that were formulated for the study and the rational of these hypotheses.

The selection of sample includes the sampling techniques used, reasons for the selection of a particular sampling technique, and the selection of sample according to different variables.

The selection of tool includes the selection of suitable tool for collection of data, description of the tool selected, testing its suitability for the present study, and the procedures followed in administering the tool to collect the data required for the present study.

OPERATIONAL DEFINITION OF KEY TERMS

The operational definitions of important terms that were used in the present study are discussed and defined herewith:

1. Attitude

Attitude is responsible for behaving in a particular and defined way. If one keeps a positive and favourable attitude towards objects, he will be attracted towards it, he will admire it and try to avoid it and even feel hostile to it. For example, a person having positive attitude towards democracy will respond positively to democratic practices and institutions and negatively to authoritarian procedures. His behaviour will speak out of his attitude.

2. Achievement

The term achievement can be understood as one's learning attainments, accomplishments or proficiencies in performing a given task. Achievement is directly related to the growth and development of pupils in educational situations, where teaching and learning go hand-in-hand. The concept of achievement involves the interaction of three factors, viz., aptitude for learning, readiness for learning and opportunity for learning. The concept also involves health and physical fitness, motives and desires and emotional balances of the individuals in the fulfillment of the given tasks. Achievement in education implies one's knowledge, understanding or skills in a specified subject or a group of subjects.

3. Social Studies

The Social Studies is concerned with man and his interaction with social and physical environment as it deals with human relations. One of the key functions of the Social Studies is to develop democratic citizenship. Before the recommendations of the Mudaliar (Secondary Education) Commission, History, Geography, Civics and Economics were taught as independent disciplines. But this commission has recommended all these social sciences should be taught under a single name called Social Studies. Since then, the subject Social Studies is being considered as a single subject at the school level with the subjects History, Geography, Civics and Economics.

4. Secondary Schools

Secondary school is a public or private school providing instruction at the level of secondary education including 8th, 9th, and 10th classes.

5. Attitude Towards Social Studies

The attitude of individuals towards Social Studies.

6. Achievement in Social Studies

The achievement of a student in the school subject Social Studies.

7. Rural Schools

The schools located in rural areas are rural schools.

8. Urban Schools

The schools located in urban areas are urban school.

9. English Medium Schools

The schools offering instruction in English medium are English medium schools.

10. Telugu Medium Schools

The schools offering instruction in Telugu medium are Telugu medium schools.

11. Private Schools

Private schools here mean the schools that are managed by private organizations or persons, either partially or totally. So, the schools managed by individuals or private agencies are considered under private schools.

12. Government Schools

The schools under the sole management of the government are government schools. So, the schools managed by zilla parishads, municipalities and government are included in this category.

VARIABLES OF THE STUDY

Variables are necessary things for any worthwhile research for the purpose of comparison. For the present study, the variables considered are Boys versus Girls, Private school students versus Government school students, Urban school students versus Rural school students and English medium school students versus Telugu medium school students.

1. Boys *Versus* Girls

In olden days, the boys were educated and the girls were restricted to their kitchens by their adult community. Times changed and the adults and the educators have recognized the importance of women education. In due course of time, women education gained importance and many parents are encouraging their daughters to pursue higher education. The women are also showing excellence in all fields. Their presence is felt almost in all fields. As the physiological conditions, exposure to society, education and other aspects of girls and boys very differently, there may be a significant difference in the possession of attitude towards Social Studies and achievement in Social Studies. The boys may be exposed to the society to a larger extent, but the girls spend most of their time in going through books or helping their parents at home. These factors may show some influence on their mental development and attitude towards Social Studies and achievement in Social Studies.

2. Private School Students *Versus* Government School Students

The reputation of private schools is generally better when compared with the government schools. In private schools, the pupils are exposed to better educational conditions and better study atmosphere. The school laboratory, library facilities, etc., will be better. If better facilities are not provided in private schools, the parents will question the authorities concerned, because they pay higher fees for their children. The laboratory and library facilities will play a major role in the possession of attitude towards Social Studies and achievement in Social Studies. The quality of teaching is also supposed to be better in private schools. The teachers take more interest in teaching in private schools as they are always either in the fear of losing their jobs or immediately being questioned by the managements about the quality of their teaching. Since the standard of teaching is supposedly is different in private and government schools, this may have influence on the attitude of students towards science and hence this variable is considered for study.

3. Rural School Students *Versus* Urban School Students

The urban schools are well equipped in many aspects when compared with the rural schools, the buildings, the libraries, the laboratories, the teaching staff, the educational atmosphere, the competitive sprit among the pupils, the amenities provided to pursue education, the exposure to fairs, exhibitions, workshops, the student participation in teaching learning process, the use of audio-visual aids, the library and laboratory facilities. The use of audio-visual aids in teaching, and the good teachers will play a commendable role in the acquisition of attitude towards Social Studies and achievement in Social Studies. A comparison between rural and urban school students will bring out the difference in the level of attitude towards Social Studies and achievement in Social Studies, if there is any which may be corrected.

4. English Medium School Students *Versus* Telugu Medium School Students

The English medium schools are thoroughly equipped with all instructional facilities when compared with the Telugu medium schools. The teaching learning process that is different in English and Telugu media schools will play a commendable role in the acquisition and development of attitude towards Social Studies and achievement in Social Studies. A comparison between English medium and Telugu medium school students will bring out the difference in the level of attitude towards Social Studies and achievement in Social Studies and necessary steps can be taken up if needed.

HYPOTHESES OF THE STUDY

Hypothesis is a tentative conclusion intended for verification. The following hypotheses were formulated based on the variables of the study. These hypotheses were stated in null form. A null hypothesis states that there is no significant difference or relationship between two or more variables. It concerns to a judgment as to whether apparent differences or relationships are true or whether they merely result from sampling errors. The following are the hypotheses of the present study:

Hypothesis 1: Secondary school pupils are not possessing high attitude towards Social Studies.

Hypothesis 1A: There is no significant difference in the level of attitude towards Social Studies of boys and girls of secondary schools.

Hypothesis 1B: There is no significant difference in the level of attitude towards Social Studies of rural and urban secondary school students.

Hypothesis 1C: There is no significant difference in the level of attitude towards Social Studies of private and government secondary school students.

Hypothesis 1D: There is no significant difference in the level of attitude towards Social Studies of English medium and Telugu medium secondary school students.

Hypothesis 2: Secondary school students are not possessing high achievement in Social Studies.

Hypothesis 2A: There is no significant difference in the level of achievement in Social Studies of boys and girls of secondary schools.

Hypothesis 2B: There is no significant difference in the level of achievement in Social Studies of rural and urban secondary school students.

Hypothesis 2C: There is no significant difference in the level of achievement in Social Studies of private and government secondary school students.

Hypothesis 2D: There is no significant difference in the level of achievement in Social Studies of English medium and Telugu medium secondary school students.

Hypothesis 3: There is no significant association between attitude towards Social Studies and achievement in Social Studies of secondary school students.

Hypothesis 3A: There is no significant association between attitude towards Social Studies and achievement in Social Studies of boys and girls of secondary schools.

Hypothesis 3B: There is no significant association between attitude towards Social Studies and achievement in Social Studies of rural and urban secondary school students.

Hypothesis 3C: There is no significant association between attitude towards Social Studies and achievement in Social Studies of private and government secondary school students.

Hypothesis 3D: There is no significant association between attitude towards Social Studies and achievement in Social Studies of English medium and Telugu medium secondary school students.

SAMPLE OF THE STUDY

After finalizing the variables of the present study, consideration was given to whether the entire population is to be made the subject for data collection or a particular group is to be selected as representative of the whole population. The entire population here refers to all the tenth class pupils of the secondary schools of Guntur district.

Of the above two techniques, the selection of group as a representative of the whole population was found to be more convenient and suitable. This technique leads to considerable saving of time, effort and finance. The number of pupils selected will be small and so it is possible to make a detailed and intensive study. This generally leads to more accurate and reliable results. As this sampling technique has many advantages, it was selected for the collection of data.

In any social research, various methods are utilized for selection and drawing of samples. After a detailed study of all these methods and considering the variables selected for the research work, the stratified sampling method was found to be most suitable. (Bhaskara Rao, D.)

In the stratified sampling method, the entire population will be divided in to smaller homogeneous groups or strata, and then a sample is selected within each group. Every sampling unit in the population is placed in one of the strata prior to the selection of the sample so that the sum of the strata is identical with the population.

Stratified sampling method has certain merits and advantages as a technique of sampling. Auckoff has rightly said that stratified sampling enables the research to make a comparison of properties of the strata as well as to estimate population characteristics.

In this stratified sampling method, the investigator has grater control over the selection of the sample when compared with random sampling. In random sampling, although every group has a chance of being selected and included in the sample, there is every possibility, and sometimes it does happen, that certain important groups are left unrepresented. But, in stratified sampling method, no important group is likely to be left out of the sample of the study.

Stratified sampling method is the ideal one when comparison between different variables has to be made. For example, if comparison has to be made between private and government school students or rural and urban students, it would be very difficult to select the required number of units through any other method of sampling. If any other method is used, the problem of bias and prejudice creeps in.

Replacement of units is also possible in the stratified sampling method. Normally, if a particular unit is not accessible for the study, it is difficult to replace it by another, but in this method it is possible. Stephen states that stratification automatically brings about a replacement of persons lost to the sample, by persons of the same stratum, thus partly correcting the bias that would result if there were no replacement of loses.

In stratified sampling method, much depends on stratification process. The following precautions were taken while stratifying the population: the variables involved in the study were taken note of, care was taken to see that each stratum in the universe was large enough in size so that each stratum of items could be done on random basis, the strata formed were defined and clear cut, each stratum was free from influence of the other; and that there was no overlapping.

Before actually selecting the sample, certain fundamental principles were also considered to make the sample scientific and clear-cut.

Firstly, the 'universe' was clearly defined. In the technical phraseology of research, the whole population out of which the samples are selected is known as the 'universe'. For the present research work, the universe includes all the students of tenth class studying in secondary schools of Andhra Pradesh. The study was limited to a particular geographical area, viz., Guntur district, to facilitate appropriate sample selection and avoid unnecessary bias and prejudice.

According to the second principle, decision has to be made about the units of the sample. A unit of sample may be a house, a family, and a group of individuals or a single individual. A good unit should possess the following characteristics: 1. *Clarity*: The unit should be clearly defined in unambiguous terms. This would make the study easy and efficient. For the present research work, a sampling unit is defined as a student of tenth class studying in any secondary school of Guntur district; 2. *Suitability*: A good unit should be well suited to the problem under study. Since the problem is on the identification of level of attitude towards social studies and achievement in social studies of tenth class students, the unit selected is well suited to the problem; 3. *Accessibility*: The unit selected should be easily accessible to the researcher. If the units selected are difficult to reach and if he fails to make use of them the study vitiated. The selected sampling unit, i.e., tenth class student is easily accessible since he\she could be approached in any secondary school.

Besides considering these principles, it is extremely important to think about the size of the sample to be selected. If the sample is either too small or too large, it will make the study difficult and also make the results untenable. According to Parten, an optimum sample in survey is one which fulfills the requirements of effective representativeness, reliability and flexibility. The size of the sample was decided after considering the following factors:

(i) Since a detailed study was planned, a very large number of samples were not selected. In case of an intensive study, very large number of samples is not so useful as they involve huge consumption of resources. A smaller sample was found to be convenient;

(ii) The size and selection of the sample will also be influenced by the nature of the universe. If the universe is homogeneous, even a small-sized sample may yield dependable and required results. If the universe is homogeneous, small-sized samples will not be useful. In case of the present study, the heterogeneous universe was split into smaller homogeneous strata and the samples were selected from these strata. For example, all the tenth class students of Guntur district will be broadly grouped under rural and urban students. A required sample will be selected from each of these groups;

(iii) The researcher needs to determine the number of groups to be formed. In case the number of groups proposed is large, the size of the sample shall have to be large that every group should be of proper size and suit to the requirements of the study. In case the number of groups proposed is small, even small-sized samples can fulfill the requirement. In case of the present study, the universe was divided in to girls and boys, private and government school students, and rural and urban school students and English medium and Telugu medium school students. Since the number of groups was more, a reasonable large sample was selected from each of these groups;

(iv) Practical considerations and accuracy also play a vital role in determining the size of the sample. Every study is guided by certain practical considerations such as time, resources, accessibility of the data, etc. Generally, it is believed that a large-sized sample is more representative and usually produces accurate results. If the sampling technique is scientific, even small-sized samples can produce dependable and accurate results. While selecting sample, the availability of resources and time were also taken into consideration. Care was taken to make the sample selection technique as scientific as possible;

(vi) The size of the sample is also governed by the size of the tools to be used. In case, the tools are short and the questions used pertain to certain limited factors, a large sample can be selected. In case, the tools are large and the questions complicated, the sample should be small in size so that, from administrative point of view, the researcher may not be put to unnecessary troubles. In the present study, the tool selected was quite elaborate and to think carefully to attend to it, hence a very large sample was not selected;

(vii) The sampling method also determines the size of the sample. When random sampling method is used, the samples have to be large. On the other hand, if samples are selected through stratified sampling method, the reliability can be achieved even with the help of the small sized samples.

Taking into consideration all these factors which influence the size of the sample, it was decided that an ideal sample would consist of two hundred students. This sample is small enough to avoid unnecessary expenditure and large enough to avoid intolerable sampling errors.

After deciding about the sampling method and the size of the sample, the universe selected was decided into different strata. The variables chosen for the study were considered to divide the universe. The variables chosen were boys versus girls, private versus government school students, urban versus rural school students and English medium and Telugu medium secondary school students.

To select the sample, all the units from all types of secondary schools were given equal importance. The individual observation or individuals are chosen in such a way as each one has an equal change of being selected, and that each choice is independent of any other choice. Random sampling may be done with the help of many methods. The lottery method suggested by Best was selected in this study.

The total sample, when split variable-wise, includes rural school students 160 and urban school students 160, government school students 160 and private school students 160 and girls 160 and boys 160, and English medium 160 and Telugu medium 160 tenth class students studying in secondary schools.

TOOL OF THE STUDY

Research tools are the sole factors in determining the sound data and in drawing accurate conclusions about the problem on hand. The conclusions ultimately help in providing suitable remedial measures to the problem concerned.

The selection and use of tools can be done in two ways. The first one is to construct a tool independently by the researcher for own study. The second way of selection and use of tool is right selection of tool from already standardized ones available in the field of study. Here also it involves a tedious job in locating the tools and identifying their usefulness to the study on hand. Even then, this technique is very useful when a research work involves a good number of variables and resources are scarce. Some people believe that some of the instruments available don't measure up to their standards. Hence, new ones. In some instances, consideration should be given to the logic of the situation. Lacking the time and financial resources, many researchers cannot expect to produce a better instrument. In these cases, the most logical procedure that one can follow is to choose the best instrument available for the purpose.

Considering the flaws and merits of the selection of tools either way, the researcher is interested in constructing a tool to measure the attitude towards Social Studies as there was no standardized achievement test to meet the requirements of the present study. To measure the achievement in Social Studies, marks of public examination in Social Studies will be taken into consideration as the examination was conducted by the Board of the Secondary Education, Government of Andhra Pradesh. The marks will effectively serve the research purpose.

Attitude towards Social Studies

A rating scale to measure attitude towards Social Studies with 40 statements has been standardized by the researchers and was administered on the sample personally and got the data from them.

Achievement in Social Studies

The marks in Social Studies obtained in Public Examination by the sample have been collected from the schools to measure the achievement of students in Social Studies.

4

ANALYSIS OF THE DATA

The organization, analysis and interpretation of data and formulation of conclusions are necessary steps to get a meaningful picture out of the raw information collected. The analysis and interpretation of data involve the objective material in the possession of the researcher and his subjective reactions and desires to derive from the data the inherent meanings in their relation to the problem.

Analysis of data means studying the tabulated material in order to determine inherent facts or meanings. It involves breaking down the existing complex factors into simple parts and putting the parts together in new arrangements for the purpose of interpretation.

After the data collection was finished, it was analyzed keeping in view the objectives and hypotheses of the study. The mean scores were used to identify the level of attitude towards Social Studies and achievement in Social Studies and to compare the sub-sample variation. The values of standard deviation were used to measure the spread or dispersion of scores in the sample distribution. The null hypotheses formulated for this study were accepted or rejected with values of critical ratio.

Hypothesis 1

The secondary school students are not possessing high attitude towards Social Studies.

To test the validity of this hypothesis, the total scores of the sample were used to calculate the mean and S.D. The results are as follows:

Table 4.1

Level of Attitude towards Social Studies Possessed by the Whole Sample

Sample	*Size*	*Mean*	*Standard Deviation*
Whole	320	76.4	5.60

As per the mean value of the whole sample, the secondary school students were possessing high attitude towards Social Studies.

The hypothesis that "the secondary school students are not possessing high attitude towards Social Studies" can be rejected.

Hypothesis 2

There is no significant difference in the level of attitude towards Social Studies of boys and girls of secondary schools.

To test the validity of the hypothesis, the critical ratio was calculated. The result is as follows:

Table 4.1A

Comparison of Attitude Towards Social Studies Between Boys and Girls of Secondary School

Variable	*Sample Size*	*Mean*	*S.D*	*Mean Difference*	*Critical Ratio*
Boys	160	76.1	5.44	0.7	1.13*
Girls	160	76.8	5.70		

* **Not Significant at 0.05 level.**

From the above table, it is evident that there is no significant difference in the attitude towards Social Studies of Boys and Girls. They were having a little high attitude towards Social Studies.

So, the hypothesis that "There is no significant difference in the level of attitude towards Social Studies of boys and girls of secondary schools" can be accepted.

Hypothesis 1B

There is no significant difference in the level of attitude towards Social Studies of rural and urban secondary school students.

The following calculations were made to test the validity of hypothesis 1B. The results are as follows:

Table 4.1B

Comparison of Attitude Towards Social Studies Between Urban and Rural Secondary School Students

Variable	*Sample Size*	*Mean*	*S.D.*	*Mean Difference*	*Critical Ratio*
Urban	160	76.80	5.80	0.7	1.12*
Rural	160	76.10	5.40		

* **Not Significant at 0.05 Level.**

From the above table, it is evident that there is no significant difference in the attitude towards Social Studies of urban and rural secondary school students. The pupils were having high level of attitude towards Social Studies.

The hypothesis that "There is no significant difference in level of attitude towards Social Studies of rural and urban secondary school students" can be accepted.

Hypothesis 1C

There is no significant difference in the level of attitude towards Social Studies of private and government secondary school students.

To test the validity of hypothesis 1C, the following calculations are made:

Table 4.1C

Comparison of Attitude Towards Social Studies Between Government and Private Secondary School Students

Variable	*Sample Size*	*Mean*	*S.D.*	*Mean Difference*	*Critical Ratio*
Govt.	160	76.50	5.40	0.20	0.32*
Private	160	76.30	5.77		

* **Not Significant at 0.05 level.**

From the above table, it is evident that there is no significant difference in the attitude towards Social Studies of government and private secondary school students.

The hypothesis that "there is no significant difference between the level of attitude towards Social Studies of private and government secondary school students" can be accepted.

Hypothesis 1D

There is no significant difference in the level of attitude towards Social Studies of English Medium and Telugu Medium secondary school students.

To test the validity of hypothesis 1D, the following calculations are made:

Table 4.1D

Comparison of Attitude Towards Social Studies Between English Medium and Telugu Medium Secondary School Students

Variable	*Sample Size*	*Mean*	*S.D.*	*Mean Difference*	*Critical Ratio*
English Medium	160	77.10	5.50	1.40	1.98*
Telugu Medium	160	75.70	5.57		

* **Not Significant at 0.05 level.**

From the above table, it is evident that there is no significant difference in the attitude towards Social Studies of English Medium and Telugu Medium secondary school students.

The hypothesis that "there is no significant difference between the level of attitude towards Social Studies of English Medium and Telugu Medium secondary school students" can be accepted.

Hypothesis 2

The secondary school students are not possessing high achievement in Social Studies.

To test the hypothesis, the total scores of all the samples were used to calculate the mean and S.D. The results are as follows:

Table 4.2
Level of Achievement Towards Social Studies by the Whole Sample

Sample	*Size*	*Mean*	*Standard Deviation*
Whole	320	73.85	14.15

As per the mean value of the whole sample, the secondary school students are possessing high achievement in Social Studies.

The hypothesis that "the secondary school students are not possessing high achievement in Social Studies" can be accepted.

Hypothesis 2A

There is no significant difference in the level of achievement in Social Studies of boys and girls of secondary schools.

The following statistical statement is to test the validity of the above hypothesis:

Table 4.2A

Comparison of Achievement in Social Studies Between Boys and Girls of Secondary School

Variable	*Size*	*Mean*	*S.D.*	*Mean Difference*	*Critical Ratio*
Boys	160	75.07	13.80	2.46	1.56*
Girls	160	72.62	14.43		

* **Not Significant at 0.05 level.**

From the above table, it is evident that there is no significant difference of the achievement in Social Studies of boys and girls. Boys were having a little bit high achievement in Social Studies.

The hypothesis that "there is no significant difference in the level of achievement in Social Studies of boys and girls of secondary school students" can be accepted.

Hypothesis 2B

There is no significant difference in the level of achievement in Social Studies of rural and urban secondary school students.

The following calculations were made to test the validity of hypotheses 2B. The results are as follows:

Table 4.2B

Comparison of Achievement in Social Studies Between Urban and Rural Secondary School Students

Variable	*Size*	*Mean*	*S.D.*	*Mean Difference*	*Critical Ratio*
Urban	160	73.04	14.71	1.61	1.02*
Rural	160	74.65	13.57		

* **Not Significant at 0.05 level.**

From the above table, it is evident that there is no significant difference in the achievement in Social Studies of urban and rural secondary school students. Urban students were having a little bit of high level of achievement in Social Studies than rural students.

The hypothesis that, "there is no significant difference in the level of achievement in Social Studies of urban and rural secondary school students" can be accepted.

Hypothesis 2C

There is no significant difference in the level of achievement in Social Studies of private and government secondary school students.

To test the validity of hypothesis 2C, the following calculations are made:

Table 4.2C

Comparison of Achievement in Social Studies Between Government and Private Secondary School Students

Variable	*Sample Size*	*Mean*	*S.D.*	*Mean Difference*	*Critical Ratio*
Govt.	160	71.64	14.39	4.41	2.82*
Private	160	76.05	13.60		

* **Significant at 0.05 level.**

From the above table, it is evident that there is a significant difference in the achievement in Social Studies of government and private secondary school students.

The hypothesis that "there is no significant difference in the level of achievement in Social Studies of private and government secondary school students" can be rejected.

Hypothesis 2D

There is no significant difference in the level of achievement in Social Studies of English Medium and Telugu medium secondary school students.

To test the validity of hypothesis 2D, the following calculations are made:

Table 4.2D

Comparison of Achievement in Social Studies Between English Medium and Telugu Medium Secondary School Students

Variable	*Sample Size*	*Mean*	*S.D.*	*Mean Difference*	*Critical Ratio*
English Medium	160	76.60	13.39	5.51	3.55*
Telugu Medium	160	71.09	14.39		

* **Significant at 0.05 level.**

From the above table, it is evident that there is a significant difference in the achievement in Social Studies of English Medium and Telugu medium secondary school students.

So, the hypothesis that "there is no significant difference in the level of achievement in Social Studies of English Medium and Telugu Medium secondary school students" can be rejected.

Hypothesis 3

There is no significant association between attitude towards Social Studies and achievement in Social Studies of secondary school students.

The following statistical statement is given to test the validity of the above hypothesis:

Table 4.3

Association of the Attitude Towards Social Studies and Achievement in Social Studies of Secondary School Students

Variable	*Sample Size*	*Mean*	*S.D*	*Correlation*
Attitude towards Social Studies	320	76.40	5.59	0.29*
Achievement in Social Studies	320	73.85	14.15	

* **Not significant at 0.05 level.**

From above table, and there was no significant association between attitude towards Social Studies and achievement in Social Studies.

The hypothesis that "there is no significant association between attitude towards Social Studies and achievement in Social Studies of secondary school students" can be accepted.

Hypothesis 3A

There is no significant association between attitude towards Social Studies and achievement in Social Studies of boys and girls of secondary schools.

To test the validity of hypothesis 3a, the following calculations are made:

Table 4.3A

Association of Attitude Towards Social Studies and Achievement in Social Studies Between Boys and Girls of Secondary School Students

<table>
<tr><th></th><th>Variable</th><th>Sample Size</th><th>Mean</th><th>S.D</th><th>Correlation</th><th>C.R</th></tr>
<tr><td rowspan="2">Boys</td><td>Attitude towards Social Studies</td><td>160</td><td>76.10</td><td>05.43</td><td rowspan="2">0.31</td><td rowspan="4">0.29*</td></tr>
<tr><td>Achievement in Social Studies</td><td>160</td><td>75.08</td><td>13.80</td></tr>
<tr><td rowspan="2">Girls</td><td>Attitude towards Social Studies</td><td>160</td><td>76.80</td><td>05.70</td><td rowspan="2">0.28</td></tr>
<tr><td>Achievement in Social Studies</td><td>160</td><td>72.62</td><td>14.43</td></tr>
</table>

* **Not Significant at 0.05 level.**

As per the table values, there was no significant association between attitude towards Social Studies and achievement in Social Studies of boys and girls of secondary schools.

The hypothesis that "there is no significant association between attitude towards Social Studies and achievement in Social Studies of boys and girls of secondary schools" can be accepted.

Hypothesis 3B

There is no significant association between attitude towards Social Studies and achievement in Social Studies of rural and urban secondary school students.

The following statistical statement is given to test the validity of above hypothesis:

Table 4.3B

Association of Attitude Towards Social Studies and Achievement in Social Studies Between Rural and Urban Area Secondary School Students

	Variable	*Sample Size*	*Mean*	*S.D*	*Correlation*	*C.R*
Rural	Attitude towards Social Studies	160	76.10	05.39	0.41	2.16*
	Achievement in Social Studies	160	74.65	13.60		
Urban	Attitude towards Social Studies	160	76.80	05.80	0.19	
	Achievement in Social Studies	160	73.04	14.71		

* **Significant 0.05 level.**

There was a significant association between attitude towards Social Studies and achievement in Social Studies of rural and urban secondary school students.

The hypothesis that "there is no significant association between attitude towards Social Studies and achievement in Social Studies of rural and urban area secondary school students" can be rejected.

Hypothesis 3C

There is no significant association between attitude towards Social Studies and achievement in Social Studies of private and government secondary school students.

To test the validity of hypothesis 3C, the following calculations are made:

Table 4.3C

Association of Attitude Towards Social Studies and Achievement in Social Studies Between Government and Private Secondary School Students

	Variable	*Sample Size*	*Mean*	*S.D*	*Correlation*	*C.R*
Govt.	Attitude towards Social Studies	160	76.50	05.40	0.31	0.29*
	Achievement in Social Studies	160	71.64	14.39		
Private	Attitude towards Social Studies	160	76.30	05.77	0.28	
	Achievement in Social Studies	160	76.05	13.60		

* **Not Significant at 0.05 level.**

The critical ratio value of two correlation values among government and private secondary school students was not significant.

The hypothesis that, "there is no significant association between attitude towards Social Studies and achievement in Social Studies of government and private secondary school students" can be accepted.

Hypothesis 3D

There is no significant association between attitude towards Social Studies and achievement in Social Studies of English Medium and Telugu medium secondary school students.

To test the validity of hypothesis 3D, the following calculations are made:

Table 4.3D

Association Between Attitude Towards Social Studies and Achievement in Social Studies of English Medium and Telugu Medium Secondary School Students

	Variable	*Sample Size*	*Mean*	*S.D*	*Correlation*	*C.R*
English Medium	Attitude towards Social Studies	160	77.10	05.50	0.44	3.12*
	Attitude in Social Studies	160	76.60	13.40		
Teluge Medium	Attitude towards Social Studies	160	75.70	05.57	0.12	
	Achievement in Social Studies	160	71.10	14.40		

* **Significant at 0.05 level.**

The critical ratio value of two correlation value among English Medium and Telugu Medium school students was not significant.

The hypothesis that "there is no significant association between attitude towards Social Studies and achievement in Social Studies of English medium and Telugu medium secondary school students" can be rejected.

5

SUMMARY, CONCLUSIONS AND DISCUSSION

SUMMARY

On 15th August 1947, India awoke to life with independence and freedom of educating the masses of India. Since this historic moment, the history of this country has been written as much in her classrooms as in her parliament. For this huge country, with its multicoloured and astonishing people, education had been both a reflection of society and an instrument of change.

It is true that the schools do not participate directly in social change; but they necessarily assume the task of preparing children for adult citizenship that involves such participation. They surely can lay the intellectual foundation for an understanding of what democracy means and what it demands of its citizenship for effecting a change in the human sector, and hence necessary training on the right lines must be given in the formative period of life in schools.

The Social Studies programme is an avenue for fostering attitudes, skills, understandings and competencies that are so essential to effect everyday-living in the society. A purposeful programme must be comprehensive and current in structure to achieve its desired objectives. Constant evaluation is necessary for the improvement of the Social Studies programmes.

As the pursuers of Social Studies are encouraged to work out a reasonable compromise between personal desires and social responsibilities, teachers of Social Studies should attempt to freedom the range of their interests by expressing to pupils about the places and issues beyond the parochial limits of the school and the community.

Considering the importance, as explained, attitude towards Social Studies and achievement in Social Studies of secondary school students are taken into consideration for a detailed study. The results of this study will help in finding out the attitude towards Social Studies and achievement in Social Studies and also their interrelationship.

Statement of the Research Problem

"A Study of Attitude towards Social Studies and achievement in Social Studies of Secondary School Students"

Need for the Study

This study helps in identifying the attitude of secondary school students towards Social Studies and their achievement in Social Studies; both are to be known necessary as Social Studies in one of the compulsory subjects of school education.

Scope of the Study

Social Studies is one of the compulsory subjects at secondary school level. It prepares good citizens besides fulfilling many aims and objectives of education. Considering the very role of Social Studies education in human living, the present study is limited to the study of attitude towards Social Studies and achievement in Social Studies of secondary school students. This study is confined to 10th class students studying the secondary schools of Guntur district.

Objectives of the Study

The following objectives are framed the present study:

1. To find out the level of attitude towards Social Studies and achievement in Social Studies of secondary school students;

2. To compare the level of attitude towards Social Studies and achievement in Social Studies between boys and girls, rural and urban students, English medium and Telugu medium students and private and government secondary school students;
3. To find out the association between attitude towards Social Studies and achievement in Social Studies of secondary school students;
4. To compare the association between attitude towards Social Studies and achievement in Social Studies of boys and girls rural and urban students, English medium and Telugu medium students and private and government secondary school students.

Method of Research

The present study involves normative survey method. The investigator selected this method because this study is an only status study.

Variables of the Study

A variable, as the name implies, is something which varies. From this point of view, a variable may be defined as those characteristics attributed to objects, events and things which can be measured. For the present study, the variables considered are: 1. Boys vs. Girls; 2. Rural secondary school students vs. urban secondary school students; 3. Government secondary school students vs. Private secondary school students; and 4. English medium school students vs. Telugu medium school students

Hypotheses of the Study

Hypothesis is a tentative conclusion intended for verification. The following hypotheses are formulated based on the variables of the study. These hypotheses are stated in null form. A null hypothesis states that there is no significant difference or relationship between two or more variables. It concerns to a judgment as to weather apparent differences or relationships are true or weather them merely from sampling errors.

Hypothesis 1: The secondary school students are not possessing high attitude towards Social Studies.

Hypothesis 1A: There is no significant difference in the level of attitude towards Social Studies of boys and girls of secondary schools.

Hypothesis 1B: There is no significant difference in the level of attitude towards Social Studies of rural and urban secondary school students.

Hypothesis 1C: There is no significant difference in the level of attitude towards Social Studies of private and government secondary school students.

Hypothesis 1D: There is no significant difference in the level of attitude towards Social Studies of English Medium and Telugu Medium secondary school students.

Hypothesis 2: The secondary school students are not possessing high achievement in Social Studies.

Hypothesis 2A: There is no significant difference in the level of achievement in Social Studies of boys and girls of secondary schools.

Hypothesis 2B: There is no significant difference in the level of achievement in Social Studies of rural and urban secondary school students.

Hypothesis 2C: There is no significant difference in the level of achievement in Social Studies of private and government secondary school students.

Hypothesis 2D: There is no significant difference in the level of achievement in Social Studies of English Medium and Telugu medium secondary school students.

Hypothesis 3: There is no significant association between attitude towards Social Studies and achievement in Social Studies of secondary school students.

Hypothesis 3A: There is no significant association between attitude towards Social Studies and achievement in Social Studies of boys and girls of secondary schools.

Hypothesis 3B: There is no significant association between attitude towards Social Studies and achievement in Social Studies of rural and urban secondary school students.

Hypothesis 3C: There is no significant association between attitude towards Social Studies and achievement in Social Studies of private and government secondary school students.

Hypothesis 3D: There is no significant association between attitude towards Social Studies and achievement in Social Studies of English Medium and Telugu medium secondary school students.

Sample of the Study

Stratified random sampling technique was found to be the most appropriate technique for the present study. Through stratified random sampling only it is possible to devide the sample into different groups or strata and choose students from each of these groups. A sample of 320 was selected for this study. Equal weightage was given to the sub-samples of variables.

Tools of the Study

For the present study, a rating scale called Attitude towards Social Studies was standardized and used to gather data to measure the level of attitude towards Social Studies. To measure the achievement in Social Studies, the marks of public examination in Social Studies were taken into consideration as the examination was conducted in the entire state by the Board of Secondary Education, Government of Andhra Pradesh.

After the data collection was completed, it was analyzed keeping in view of the objectives of the present study.

CONCLUSIONS AND DISCUSSION

The present study has resulted in drawing the following conclusions which may be utilized in improving the attitude towards Social Studies and achievement in Social Studies of secondary school students.

1. The Secondary School Students are Possessing High Attitude Towards Social Studies.

The secondary school students having a high attitude towards Social Studies is a welcoming sign in present-day education as several students and parents are looking towards science, technology and management subjects. The school authorities, by maintaining this attitude towards Social Studies, should support the programmes that help the students choose and settle in the valued professions of social sciences.

2. There is No Significant Difference in the Level of Attitude Towards Social Studies of Boys and Girls of Secondary Schools, Though Both of them Possess High Level of Attitude Towards Social Studies.

Now-a-days, girls are equally competing with boys in every aspect, and this might be in support of having high attitude towards Social Studies. This attitude should help the students in pursuing different courses in Social Studies at higher levels of learning. The parents and teachers should see that this attitude be maintained further to make them settle well in future careers.

3 There is No Significant Difference in the Level of Attitude Towards Social Studies of Rural and Urban Secondary School Students. Both the Samples Possess High Level of Attitude Towards Social Studies.

Several facilities and cultures that prevail in rural and urban habitations didn't show any influence on the attitude of school students towards Social Studies. This shows the strong desire of students towards the importance and learning Social Studies. The people and personnel connected with rural students and schools should help the students compete on par with urbanites in all academic as well as professional careers.

4. There is No Significant Difference in the Level of Attitude Towards Social Studies of Private and Government Secondary School Students. The Student of Government and Private Schools Possess High Level of Attitude Towards Social Studies.

Though the infrastructural and instructional facilities and also socio-cultural conditions vary significantly in private school ands government schools, the students of both the schools did possess equally high attitude towards Social Studies subject, which is a good sign to both of students and parents along with the government. The government school authorities, recognizing this attitude level, should try to provide the facilities as much as it can to promote the quality of education in government schools by utilizing the high level of attitude towards Social Studies.

5. **There is No Significant Difference in the Level of Attitude Towards Social Studies of English Medium and Telugu Medium Secondary School Students, Though Both of Them Possess High Level of Attitude Towards Social Studies.**

The medium of instruction did not exert any influence on the attitude of students towards Social Studies, though the facilities and amenities do vary significantly in English medium and Telugu medium schools. Students from both the schools hold high attitude towards Social Studies and this will help the student s do well in the subject Social Studies.

6. **The Secondary School Students are Possessing High Achievement in Social Studies.**

The secondary school students are with high achievement in Social Studies can be come good citizens and can also become successful professionals in social sciences. The teachers need to make the students aware of the vocations that satisfy the life and career of the students. The students should also maintain the same achievement throughout their academic career and do their best in achieving excellence in Social Studies.

7. **The Secondary School Boys and Girls are Having High Achievement in Social Studies. There is No Significant Difference in the Level of Achievement in Social Studies of Boys and Girls of Secondary Schools.**

The result that there is no difference in the achievement in Social Studies between the boys and girls is a welcoming sign of the academic spirit between the boys and girls. With this high achievement, both boys and girls should do their best to settle well in better jobs in social sciences.

8. **The Rural and Urban Secondary School Students are Having High Achievement in Social Studies. There is No Significant Difference in the Level of Achievement in Social Studies of Rural and Urban Secondary School Students.**

There are differences in the academic as well as personal facilities available in rural and urban localities, still the rural and urban students achieve equally in Social Studies. Both should maintain the same excellence and continue this trend in higher education also.

9. **The Private and Government Secondary School Students are Having High Achievement in Social Studies. There is a Significant Difference in the Level of Achievement in Social Studies of Private and Government Secondary School Students. The Private School Students are Superior in Achievement Than Government School Students.**

As the infrastructural and instructional facilities vary significantly in private school and government schools, the students of both the schools didn't perform equally in Social Studies; but the private school students fared well than their counter parts; which is not a good sign both of students and parents along with the government. The government school authorities, recognizing this achievement level, should try to provide the facilities as much as they can to promote the quality of education in government schools.

10. **The Telugu Medium and English Medium Secondary School Students are Having High Achievement in Social Studies. There is a Significant Difference in the Level of Achievement in Social Studies of English Medium and Telugu Medium Secondary School Students. The English Medium School Students are Superior in Achievement in Social Studies Than Telugu Medium School Students.**

The English medium school students are superior in achievement in Social Studies than Telugu medium school students, though both of them possess high achievement in Social Studies, which shows that the facilities of instruction and infrastructure have their legitimate role to play in the achievement in Social Studies. The Telugu medium students should also get these facilities to perform on par with their counterparts, and hence the managements should provide the conducive facilities for that.

11. There is No Significant Association Between Attitude Towards Social Studies and Achievement in Social Studies of Secondary School Students.

There is no significant association between attitude towards Social Studies and achievement in Social Studies of secondary school students, though the secondary school students possess a high attitude towards Social Studies and a high achievement in Social Studies. Attitude may have its influence on achievement, but, in this study, there is no such association between attitude and achievement. Whatever the result may be, the school teachers must promote both right attitude towards Social Studies and achievement in Social Studies for the benefit of the student community.

12. There is No Significant Association Between Attitude Towards Social Studies and Achievement in Social Studies of Boys and Girls of Secondary Schools.

Though the secondary school students possess a high attitude towards Social Studies and a high achievement in Social Studies, there is no significant association between attitude towards Social Studies and achievement in Social Studies of boy and girl students. This study reveals that there is no gender influence on the association between attitude and achievement, which is a welcoming phenomenon.

13. There is a Significant Association Between Attitude Towards Social Studies and Achievement in Social Studies of Rural and Urban Secondary School Students.

There is a significant association between attitude towards Social Studies and achievement in Social Studies of rural and urban secondary school students, as both the secondary school students possess high attitude towards Social Studies and high achievement in Social Studies. As there is an influence of locality on attitude and achievement, the teachers should support the students to excel in Social Studies.

14. There is No Significant Association Between Attitude Towards Social Studies and Achievement in Social Studies of Private and Government Secondary School Students.

There is no significant association between attitude towards Social Studies and achievement in Social Studies of private and government secondary school students, though both the samples possess high attitude towards Social Studies and high achievement in Social Studies. Whether there is an association between attitude towards Social Studies and achievement in Social Studies of private and government secondary school students, it is the duty of the teachers and school authorities to promote both of these traits in order to make the students pursue education in Social Studies.

15. There is a Significant Association Between Attitude Towards Social Studies and Achievement in Social Studies of English Medium and Telugu Medium Secondary School Students.

As the secondary school students possess high attitude towards Social Studies and high achievement in Social Studies, there is a significant association between attitude towards Social Studies and achievement in Social Studies of English Medium and Telugu medium secondary school students. The managements of both the schools should see that the attitude and achievement grow along with the age and class of the students and the students excel in all walks of life with this attitude towards Social Studies and achievement in Social Studies.

To conclude, the secondary school students are holding high attitude towards Social Studies and the gender, locality of the school, management of the school and medium of instruction have no influence on the attitude towards Social Studies possessed by the students. The secondary school students are possessing high achievement in Social Studies and gender and locality of the school are not having influence on the achievement in Social Studies, but management of the school and medium of instruction have their influence on the achievement in Social Studies. There is no significant association between attitude towards Social Studies and achievement in Social Studies of secondary school students and there is no influence of gender and management and there is influence of locality of the school and medium of instruction on the attitude towards Social Studies and achievement in Social Studies. The parents, teachers and students should collectively work for the retainment of the high attitude towards Social Studies and high achievement in Social Studies in order to excel in every walk of life in future and to become useful citizen of India.

SUGGESTIONS FOR FUTHER RESEARCH

The present study on attitude towards Social Studies and achievement in Social Studies brings to light a good number of new areas to be studied by the future researches. The areas and variables which are not covered by this study may be put to test to enlighten the factors associated with the inculcation and development of attitude towards Social Studies and achievement in Social Studies.

So, the researchers may think of the following areas to study in detail:

Studies on attitude towards Social Studies and achievement in Social Studies may be extended to the other educational levels-wise, primary and college levels and district as well as state levels;

Studies can be carried out on other variables like residential and non-residential system;

Studies on the effect of socio-economic status of the students in the development of attitude towards Social Studies and achievement in Social Studies of secondary school students can be taken up;

Studies may be conducted on the attitude towards and interest in Social Studies and achievement in Social Studies of secondary school students;

Studies may be carried out to find out the effect of independent variables on dependent variables in the cases of controlled and experimental groups;

Studies may be conducted on the effect of achievement motivation and personality on achievement in Social Studies;

Studies may be taken up on the effect of teachers' attitude towards Social Studies in promoting pupils' attitude towards Social Studies and achievement in Social Studies;

Studies may be taken up in other dimensions of attitude towards Social Studies and achievement in Social Studies of secondary school students.

BIBLIOGRAPHY

Aggarwal, Y.P. ***Statistical Methods,*** New Delhi: Sterling Publishing House.

Best, John W. (1982), ***Research in Education,*** 4th Edition. New Delhi: Prentice Hall of India Pvt. Ltd.

Bhaskara Rao, D., Vijaya, K. and Sridevi, C. (1995), ***Achievement in Social Studies,*** New Delhi: Discovery Publishing House.

Buch, M.B., Chief Editor (1987), ***Second Survey of Research in Education,*** New Delhi: NCERT.

Buch, M.B., Chief Editor (1989), ***Third Survey of Research in Education,*** New Delhi: NCERT.

Edger, Marlow and Bhaskara Rao, D. (2004), ***Teaching Social Studies Successfully,*** New Delhi: Discovery Publishing House.

Grewal, P.S. ***Methods of Statistical Analysis,*** New Delhi: Sterling Publishing House.

Goode, William, J. and Paul K. Hatt (1983), ***Methods in Social Research,*** New Delhi: McGraw-Hill.

Kochar, S.K. (1979). ***Teaching of Social Studies,*** New Delhi: Sterling Publishers Pvt. Ltd.

Lohithaksh (2003), ***Dictionary of Education—A Practical Approach,*** New Delhi: Kanishka Publishing and Distributors.

Nibedita, Das (2004), ***Fundamentals of Teaching***, New Delhi: Dominant Publishing and Distributors.

Rummel, Frances J. (1958), ***An Introduction to Research Procedure in Education***, New York: Harper and Brothers.

Sidhu, K.S. (1984), ***Methodology of Research in Education***, New Delhi: Sterling Publishing House.

REFERENCES

Bhaskara Rao, Digumarti (1994), ***Scientific Aptitude***, New Delhi: Ashish Publishing House. ISBN 81-7024-658-X.

Bhaskara Rao, Digumarti (1995), ***Animal Kingdom***, New Delhi: Discovery Publishing House. ISBN 81-7141-274-2.

Bhaskara Rao, Digumarti (1995), ***Batracology***, New Delhi: Discovery Publishing House. ISBN 81-7141-279-3.

Bhaskara Rao, Digumarti (1997), ***Scientific Attitude***, New Delhi: Discovery Publishing House. ISBN 81-7141-381-1.

Bhaskara Rao, Digumarti (1996), ***Scientific Attitude vis-à-vis Scientific Aptitude***, New Delhi: Discovery Publishing House. ISBN 81-7141-308-0.

Bhaskara Rao, Digumarti (2004), ***Scientific Attitude, Scientific Aptitude and Achievement***, New Delhi: Discovery Publishing House. ISBN 81-7141-781-7.

Bhaskara Rao, Digumarti (2004), ***Educational Administration***, New Delhi: Discovery Publishing House. ISBN 81-7141-842-2.

Bhaskara Rao, Digumarti (2004), ***Issues in School Education***, New Delhi: Discovery Publishing House. ISBN 81-8356-025-3.

Bhaskara Rao, Digumarti, Editor (1996), ***Encyclopaedia of Education For All***, 5 Volumes. New Delhi: APH Publishing Corporation. ISBN 81-7024-759-4 (Set).

Vol. I ***Education For All: The World Conference***, ISBN 81-7024-760-8

Vol. II ***Education For All: The EPA-9 Summit***, ISBN 81-7024-761-6.

Vol. III *Education For All: Quality Education For All,* ISBN 81-7024-762-6.

Vol. IV *Education For All: Planning and Monitoring,* ISBN 81-7024-763-4.

Vol. V *Education For All: The Indian Scenario,* ISBN 81-7024-764-0.

Bhaskara Rao, Digumarti, Editor (1996), ***National Policy on Education,*** 2 Volumes. New Delhi: Anmol Publications Pvt. Ltd. ISBN 81-7488-323-1.

Bhaskara Rao, Digumarti, Editor (1996), ***Global Perceptions on Peace Education,*** 3 Volumes. New Delhi: Discovery Publishing House. ISBN 81-7141-319-6.

Bhaskara Rao, Digumarti, Editor (1997), ***Education for the 21st Century,*** New Delhi: Discovery Publishing House. ISBN 81-7141-389-7.

Bhaskara Rao, Digumarti, Editor (1997), ***Reflections on Scientific Attitude,*** New Delhi: Discovery Publishing House. ISBN 81-7141-319-6.

Bhaskara Rao, Digumarti, Editor (1997), ***Success Story of a Primary Education Project,*** New Delhi: APH Publishing Corporation. ISBN 81-7024-850-7.

Bhaskara Rao, Digumarti, Editor (1997), ***World Food Summit,*** New Delhi: Discovery Publishing House. ISBN 81-7141-386-2.

Bhaskara Rao, Digumarti, Editor (1997), ***Care the Child,*** 2 Volumes. New Delhi: Discovery Publishing House. ISBN 81-7141-394-3.

Bhaskara Rao, Digumarti, Editor (1998), ***Earth Summit,*** 2 Volumes. New Delhi: Discovery Publishing House. ISBN 81-7141-435-4.

Bhaskara Rao, Digumarti, Editor (1998), ***Adolescence Education,*** New Delhi: Discovery Publishing House. ISBN 81-7141-432-X.

Bhaskara Rao, Digumarti, Editor (1998), ***Community and School Nutrition Education,*** New Delhi: Discovery Publishing House. ISBN 81-7141-435-4.

Bhaskara Rao, Digumarti, Editor (1998), ***District Primary Education Programme***, New Delhi: Discovery Publishing House. ISBN 81-7141-396-X.

Bhaskara Rao, Digumarti, Editor (1998), ***National Policy on Education: Towards an Enlightened and Humane Society***, New Delhi: Discovery Publishing House. ISBN 81-7141-426-5.

Bhaskara Rao, Digumarti, Editor (1998), ***Reforming School Education***, New Delhi: Discovery Publishing House. ISBN 81-7141-403-6.

Bhaskara Rao, Digumarti, Editor (1998), ***Teacher Education in India***, New Delhi: Discovery Publishing House. ISBN 81-7141-406-0.

Bhaskara Rao, Digumarti, Editor (1998), ***World Summit for Social Development***, New Delhi: Discovery Publishing House. ISBN 81-7141-420-6.

Bhaskara Rao, Digumarti, Editor (1999), ***International Encyclopaedia of AIDS***, 11 Volumes. New Delhi: Discovery Publishing House. ISBN 81-7141-522-6 (Set).

Vol. 1 ***Introduction to HIV/AIDS***, ISBN 81-7141-523-7.

Vol. 2 ***HIV/AIDS–Issues and Challenges***, 2 Parts. ISBN 81-7141-524-5.

Vol. 3 ***HIV/AIDS–Socio Economic Realities***, ISBN 81-7141-524-3.

Vol. 4 ***HIV/AIDS–Law Ethics and Human Rights***, 2 Parts. ISBN 81-7141-526-1.

Vol. 5 ***AIDS and NGOs***, ISBN 81-7141-527-X.

Vol. 6 ***AIDS and Home Care***, ISBN 81-7141-528-8.

Vol. 7 ***STD Case Management***, ISBN 81-7141-529-6.

Vol. 8 ***HIV/AIDS Prevention and Care—Teaching Modules for Nurses and Midwives***, ISBN 81-7141-530-X.

Vol. 9 ***HIV Prevention Education for Educational Institutions***, ISBN 81-7141-531-8.

Vol.10 *Instructional Modules for AIDS Education,* ISBN 81-7141-532-6.

Vol.11 *School Health Education to Prevent AIDS* **and** *STD – A Package for Curriculum Planners,* ISBN 81-7141-533-4.

Bhaskara Rao, Digumarti, Editor (2000), *International Encyclopaedia of Human Rights,* 7 Volumes in 13 Parts. New Delhi: Discovery Publishing House. ISBN 81-7141-567-9 (set).

Vol. 1 *International Instruments of Human Rights,* 2 Parts. ISBN 81-7141-569-4.

Vol. 2 *Regional Instruments of Human Rights,* ISBN 81-7141-604-7.

Vol. 3 *Human Rights and the United Nations,* 2 Parts. ISBN 81-7141-605-5.

Vol. 4 *Fact Files of Human Rights,* 3 Parts. ISBN 81-7141-606-3.

Vol. 5 *Study Stories of Human Rights,* 3 Parts. ISBN 81-7141-607-3.

Vol. 6 *International Meetings on Human Rights,* 2 Parts. ISBN 81-714-608-X.

Vol. 7 *Professional Training in Human Rights,* ISBN 81-7141-609-8.

Bhaskara Rao, Digumarti, Editor (2000), *International Encyclopaedia of Science and Technology Education,* 11 Volumes. New Delhi: Discovery Publishing House. ISBN 81-7141-548-2 (set).

Vol. 1 *Science and Technology Education,* ISBN 81-7141-568-7.

Vol. 2 *Science Education in Developing Countries,* ISBN 81-7141-569-9.

Vol. 3 *Organizational Structure of Science,* ISBN 81-7141-570-9.

Vol. 4 *Science Education in Asia and the Pacific*, ISBN 81-7141-571-7.

Vol. 5 *Science and Technology Education For All*, ISBN 81-7141-572-5.

Vol. 6 *Values, Ethics, Talent and Girls in Science and Technology Education*, ISBN 81-7141-573-3.

Vol. 7 *Popularization of Science and Technology Education*, ISBN 81-7141-574-1.

Vol. 8 *Science, Power and Society*, ISBN 81-7141-575-X.

Vol. 9 *Information Technology*, ISBN 81-7141-576-8.

Vol. 10 *Teacher Training in Science and Technology Education*, ISBN 81-7142-577-6.

Vol. 11 *Teacher Training in Science and Technology: A Curriculum Framework*, ISBN 81-7141-578-4.

Bhaskara Rao, Digumarti, Editor (2000), ***Education For All: Achieving the Goal***, 3 Volumes. New Delhi: APH Publishing Corporation. ISBN 81-7648-152-1 (set).

Vol. I ***The Global Consensus***, ISBN 81-7648-155-6.

Vol. II ***Mid-Decade Review Reports of Regional Seminars***, ISBN 81-7648- 154-8.

Vol. III ***Issues and Trends***, ISBN 81-7648-155-6.

Bhaskara Rao, Digumarti, Editor (2001), ***Nuclear Materials: Issues and Concerns***, 2 Volumes. New Delhi: Discovery Publishing House. ISBN 81-7141-611-X.

Bhaskara Rao, Digumarti, Editor (2001), ***Distance Education in Different Countries***, New Delhi: APH Publishing Corporation. ISBN 81-7648-229-3.

Bhaskara Rao, Digumarti, Editor (2001), ***Decentralised Management of Education: Management of Education in Panchayati Raj and Municipal Bodies***, New Delhi: Discovery Publishing House. ISBN 81-7141-617-9.

Bhaskara Rao, Digumarti, Editor (2001), ***Electrochemistry for Environmental Protection***, New Delhi: Discovery Publishing House. ISBN 81-7141-619-5.

Bhaskara Rao, Digumarti, Editor (2001), ***Global Educational Studies***, New Delhi: Discovery Publishing House. ISBN 81-7141-616-0.

Bhaskara Rao, Digumarti, Editor (2001), ***Global Synthesis of Educational Assessment***, New Delhi: Discovery Publishing House. ISBN 81-7141-613-6.

Bhaskara Rao, Digumarti, Editor (2001), ***Jomtein Decade of Education***, New Delhi: Discovery Publishing House. ISBN 81-7141-618-7.

Bhaskara Rao, Digumarti, Editor (2001), ***World Conference on Education for All***, New Delhi: APH Publishing Corporation. ISBN 81-7648-274-9.

Bhaskara Rao, Digumarti, Editor (2001), ***World Conference on Higher Education***, New Delhi: Discovery Publishing House. ISBN 81-7141-610-1.

Bhaskara Rao, Digumarti, Editor (2001), ***World Conference on Science***, New Delhi: Discovery Publishing House. ISBN 81-7141-612-8.

Bhaskara Rao, Digumarti, Editor (2003), ***Inspiring Experiences in Teacher Education***, New Delhi: Discovery Publishing House. ISBN 81-7141-656-X.

Bhaskara Rao, Digumarti, Editor (2003), ***International Studies in Education***, 3 Volumes. New Delhi: Discovery Publishing House. ISBN 81-7141-647-0.

Bhaskara Rao, Digumarti, Editor (2003), ***Military Conversion: Impact on Science and Technology***, New Delhi: Discovery Publishing House. ISBN 81-7141-578-4.

Bhaskara Rao, Digumarti, Editor (2003), ***United Nations Millennium Summit***, New Delhi: Discovery Publishing House. ISBN 81-7141-632-2.

Bhaskara Rao, Digumarti, Editor (2003), ***World Assembly on Aging***, New Delhi: Discovery Publishing House. ISBN 81-7141-637-3.

Bhaskara Rao, Digumarti, Editor (2003), ***World Conference on Human Rights***, New Delhi: Discovery Publishing House. ISBN 81-7141-661-6.

Bhaskara Rao, Digumarti, Editor (2003), ***World Education Forum,*** New Delhi: Discovery Publishing House. ISBN 81-7141-639-X.

Bhaskara Rao, Digumarti, Editor (2003), ***Education, Employment and Human Resource Development,*** New Delhi: Discovery Publishing House. ISBN 81-7141-681-0.

Bhaskara Rao, Digumarti, Editor (2003), ***Successful Schooling,*** New Delhi: Discovery Publishing House. ISBN 81-7141-677-2.

Bhaskara Rao, Digumarti, Editor (2003), ***European Education and Teachers,*** New Delhi: Discovery Publishing House. ISBN 81-7141-702-7.

Bhaskara Rao, Digumarti, Editor (2003), ***Teachers in a Changing World,*** New Delhi: Discovery Publishing House. ISBN 81-7141-694-2.

Bhaskara Rao, Digumarti, Editor (2004), ***International Guidelines on Open and Distance Teacher Education,*** New Delhi: Discovery Publishing House. ISBN 81-7141-777-9.

Bhaskara Rao, Digumarti, Editor (2004), ***Adult Learning in the 21st Century,*** New Delhi: Discovery Publishing House. ISBN 81-7141-797-3.

Bhaskara Rao, Digumarti, Editor (2004), ***Educational Practices: Research and Recommendations,*** New Delhi: Discovery Publishing House. ISBN 81-7141-835-X.

Bhaskara Rao, Digumarti, Editor (2004), ***General Secondary Education In the 21st Century,*** New Delhi: Discovery Publishing House.

Bhaskara Rao, Digumarti, Editor (2004), ***International Encyclopaedia of Learning to Live Together,*** 4 Volumes. New Delhi: Discovery Publishing House. ISBN 81-7141-848-1.

Vol. 1 ***International Conference on Learning to Live Together.***

Vol. 2 ***Globalization and Living Together.***

Vol. 3 ***Curriculum for Learning to Live Together.***

Vol. 4 ***Science Education for the Contemporary Society.***

Bhaskara Rao, Digumarti, Editor (2004), ***Reforming Secondary Education,*** New Delhi: Discovery Publishing House. ISBN 81-7141-843-0.

Bhaskara Rao, Digumarti, Editor (2004), ***Human Rights Education,*** New Delhi: Discovery Publishing House. ISBN 81-7141-882-1.

Bhaskara Rao, Digumarti, Editor (2004), ***United Nations Decade for Human Rights Education,*** New Delhi: Discovery Publishing House. ISBN 81-7141-887-2.

Bhaskara Rao, Digumarti, Editor (2004), ***Technical and Vocational Education and Training in the 21st Century,*** New Delhi: Discovery Publishing House. ISBN 81-7141-984-4.

Bhaskara Rao, Digumarti, Editor (2005), ***Encyclopaedia of Education For All,*** 5 Volumes. New Delhi: Discovery Publishing House.

Bhaskara Rao, Digumarti and B.S.V. Dutt, Editors (2003), ***Education: Programmes and Policies,*** New Delhi: APH Publishing Corporation. ISBN 81-7648-470-9.

Bhaskara Rao, Digumarti, C.A.P. Swamy and B.S.V. Dutt (1997), ***Self-Evaluation in Student Teaching,*** New Delhi: Discovery Publishing House. ISBN 81-7141-374-9.

Bhaskara Rao, Digumarti and D. Naresh Kumar (2004), ***School Teacher Effectiveness,*** New Delhi: Discovery Publishing House. ISBN 81-7141-782-5.

Bhaskara Rao, Digumarti and D. Sridhar (2002), ***Job Satisfaction of School Teachers,*** New Delhi: Discovery Publishing House. ISBN 81-7141-652-7.

Bhaskara Rao, Digumarti, C. Sridevi and K. Vijaya (1995), ***Achievement in Social Studies,*** New Delhi: Discovery Publishing House. ISBN 81-7141-281-5.

Bhaskara Rao, Digumarti and Digumarti Pushpa Latha (1994), ***Achievement in Biology,*** New Delhi: Discovery Publishing House. ISBN 81-7141-264-5.

Bhaskara Rao, Digumarti and Digumarti Pushpa Latha (1995), ***Achievement in English,*** New Delhi: Discovery Publishing House. ISBN 81-7141-283-1.

Bhaskara Rao, Digumarti and Digumarti Pushpa Latha (1994), ***Achievement in Science***, New Delhi: Discovery Publishing House. ISBN 81-7141-280-7.

Bhaskara Rao, Digumarti and Digumarti Pushpa Latha (1995), ***Achievement in Mathematics***, New Delhi: Discovery Publishing House. ISBN 81-7141-278-5.

Bhaskara Rao, Digumarti and Digumarti Pushpa Latha (2004), ***Education for Women***, New Delhi: Discovery Publishing House. ISBN 81-7141-873-2.

Bhaskara Rao, Digumarti, Digumarti Pushpa Latha and Digumarthi Harshitha, Editors (2001), ***Biological Warfare***, New Delhi: Discovery Publishing House. ISBN 81-7141-597-0.

Bhaskara Rao, Digumarti, Digumarti Pushpa Latha and Digumarthi Harshitha, Editors (2001), ***Women as Educators***, New Delhi: Discovery Publishing House. ISBN 81-7141-602-0.

Bhaskara Rao, Digumarti and Digumarthi Harshitha (2004), ***Adjustment of Adolescents***, New Delhi: APH Publishing House. ISBN 81-7648-836-8.

Bhaskara Rao, Digumarti and Digumarthi Harshitha, Editors (2001), ***Education in India***, New Delhi: APH Publishing House. ISBN 81-7648-207-2.

Bhaskara Rao, Digumarti and Digumarti Pushpa Latha, Editors (1998). ***International Encyclopaedia of Women***, 5 Volumes. New Delhi: Discovery Publishing House. ISBN 81-7141-410-9 (set).

Vol. 1 ***Status of World's Women***, ISBN 81-7141-494-X.

Vol. 2 ***Women, Education and Empowerment***, ISBN 81-7141-498-1.

Vol. 3 ***Women Challenges and Advancement***, ISBN 81-7141-497-4.

Vol. 4 ***Women and Family Health***, ISBN 81-7141-497-4.

Vol. 5 ***Women and International Action***, ISBN 81-7141-498-2.

Bhaskara Rao, Digumarti, Digumarti Pushpa Latha and Digumarthi Harshitha, Editors (2001), ***Assessing Learning Achievement***, New Delhi: Discovery Publishing House. ISBN 81-7141-601-2.

Bhaskara Rao, Digumarti, Digumarti Pushpa Latha and Digumarthi Harshitha, Editors (2001), ***Energy Security***, New Delhi: Discovery Publishing House. ISBN 81-7141-598-9.

Bhaskara Rao, Digumarti, Digumarthi Harshitha and K.R.S. Sambasiva Rao, Editors (1999), ***Advanced Biotechnology***, New Delhi: Discovery Publishing House. ISBN 81-7141-516-4.

Bhaskara Rao, Digumarti and K.R.S. Sambasiva Rao, Editors (1996), ***Current Trends in Indian Education***. New Delhi: Discovery Publishing House. ISBN 81-7141-311-0.

Bhaskara Rao, Digumarti and D. Naresh Kumar (2004), ***School Teacher Effectiveness***, New Delhi: Discovery Publishing House. ISBN 81-7141-782-5.

Bhaskara Rao, Digumarti and E. Sreekanth Babu (2004), ***Educational Interests of School Students***, New Delhi: Discovery Publishing House. ISBN 81-7141-837-6.

Bhaskara Rao, Digumarti and K. Vijaya (1995), ***A Text Book Evaluation***, Ambala Cantt: The Associated Publishers.

Bhaskara Rao, Digumarti and M.A. Fayaz (2004), ***Problems of Primary School Drop-outs***, New Delhi: Discovery Publishing House. ISBN 81-7141-834-1.

Bhaskara Rao, Digumarti and N.V.M. Mohana Rao (2002), ***Problems of Mentally Handicapped Children***, New Delhi: Discovery Publishing House. ISBN 81-7141- 645-4.

Bhaskara Rao, Digumarti and S. Chandra Mohan (2002), ***Sports Management***, New Delhi: APH Publishing House. ISBN 81-7648-467-9.

Bhaskara Rao, Digumarti and S.A. Khader (2004), ***Problems of Private School Teachers***, New Delhi: Discovery Publishing House. ISBN 81-7141-838-4.

Bhaskara Rao, Digumarti and S.A. Khader (2004), ***School Education in India,*** New Delhi: Discovery Publishing House. ISBN 81-7141-849-X.

Bhaskara Rao, Digumarti and Sk. Johni Basha (2004), ***Teachers' Population Education Awareness,*** New Delhi: Discovery Publishing House. ISBN 81-7141-832-5.

Bhaskara Rao, Digumarti, V. Venkateswara Rao, V. Vijaya Lakshmi and V. Vamsi Krishna, Editors (1999). ***Status and Advancement of Women,*** New Delhi: APH Publishing Corporation. ISBN 81-7648-169-6.

Appala Naidu, P.Ch., Author and Digumarti Bhaskara Rao, Editor (2007). ***Feedback Methods and Student Performance,*** New Delhi: Discovery Publishing House. ISBN 81-8356-284-1.

Babu, P.C., Author and Digumarti Bhaskara Rao, Editor (2004). ***Flowers of Wisdom,*** New Delhi: Discovery Publishing House. ISBN 81-7141-695-0.

Bujji Babu, K., Author and Digumarti Bhaskara Rao, Editor (2007). ***Teaching Aptitude of Primary School Teachers,*** New Delhi: Sonali Publications. ISBN 81-8411-083-9.

Amala, P.A. and Anupama, P., Authors and Digumarti Bhaskara Rao, Editor (2004), ***History of Education,*** New Delhi: Discovery Publishing House. ISBN 81-7141-860-0.

Bhagya Lakshmi, L., Author and Digumarti Bhaskara Rao, Editor (2000), ***Reading and Comprehension,*** New Delhi: Discovery Publishing House. ISBN 81-7141-543-1.

Bhasha, S.A., Author and Digumarti Bhaskara Rao, Editor (2004), ***Methods of Teaching Geography,*** New Delhi: Discovery Publishing House. ISBN 81-7141-807-4.

Bhuvaneswara Lakshmi, Gadde, Author and Digumarti Bhaskara Rao, Editor (2000). ***Attitude Towards Science,*** New Delhi: Discovery Publishing House. ISBN 81-7141-541-6.

Bhuvaneswara Lakshmi, G., Author and Digumarti Bhaskara Rao, Editor (2004). ***Methods of Teaching Life Science,*** New Delhi: Discovery Publishing House. ISBN 81-7141-804-X.

Bhuvaneswara Lakshmi, G. and K. Subba Rao, Authors and Digumarti Bhaskara Rao, Editor (2004), ***Methods of Teaching Biology***, New Delhi: Discovery Publishing House. ISBN 81-7141-914-3.

Chary, K.V.N.B., Author and Digumarti Bhaskara Rao, Editor (2006), ***Techniques of Teaching Physics***, New Delhi: Sonali Publications. ISBN 81-8411-046-4.

Chowdary, S.B.J.R. and Naga Raju, Authors and Digumarti Bhaskara Rao, Editor (2004), ***Mastery of Teaching Skills***, New Delhi: Discovery Publishing House.

Dayakara Reddy, V. and Digumarti Bhaskara Rao, Editors (2006), ***Value-Oriented Education***, New Delhi: Discovery Publishing House. ISBN 81-8356-051-2.

Devraj, T.A.S., Author and Digumarti Bhaskara Rao, Editor (1997), ***Trace Analysis of Uranium and Thorium***, New Delhi: Discovery Publishing House. ISBN 81-7141-375-7.

Durga Rani, K., Author and Digumarti Bhaskara Rao, Editor (2000), ***Educational Aspirations and Scientific Attitudes***, New Delhi: Discovery Publishing House. ISBN 81-7141-555-5.

Dutt, B.S.V. and Digumarti Bhaskara Rao (2001), ***Empowering Primary Teachers***, New Delhi: Discovery Publishing House. ISBN 81-7141-615-2.

Dutt, B.S.V., Author and Digumarti Bhaskara Rao, Editor (2004), ***Comparative Education***, New Delhi: Discovery Publishing House. ISBN 81-7141-912-7.

Ediger, Marlow and Digumarti Bhaskara Rao (1996), ***Science Curriculum***, New Delhi: Discovery Publishing House. ISBN 81-7141-321-8.

Ediger, Marlow and Digumarti Bhaskara Rao (2000), ***Teaching Mathematics Successfully***, New Delhi: Discovery Publishing House. ISBN 81-7141-552-0.

Ediger, Marlow and Digumarti Bhaskara Rao (2001), ***Teaching Science Successfully***, New Delhi: Discovery Publishing House. ISBN 81-7141-600-4.

Ediger, Marlow and Digumarti Bhaskara Rao (2001), ***Teaching Social Studies Successfully***, New Delhi: Discovery Publishing House. ISBN 81-7141-596-2.

Ediger, Marlow and Digumarti Bhaskara Rao (2002), ***Philosophy and Curriculum***, New Delhi: Discovery Publishing House. ISBN 81-7141-631-4.

Ediger, Marlow and Digumarti Bhaskara Rao (2002), ***Improving School Administration***, New Delhi: Discovery Publishing House. ISBN 81-7141-633-0

Ediger, Marlow and Digumarti Bhaskara Rao (2002), ***Elementary Curriculum***, New Delhi: Discovery Publishing House. ISBN 81-7141-658-6.

Ediger, Marlow and Digumarti Bhaskara Rao (2003), ***Language Arts Curriculum***, New Delhi: Discovery Publishing House. ISBN 81-7141-657-8.

Ediger, Marlow and Digumarti Bhaskara Rao (2003), ***Psychology and Curriculum***, New Delhi: Discovery Publishing House. ISBN 81-7141-691-8.

Ediger, Marlow and Digumarti Bhaskara Rao (2003), ***Teaching Language Arts Successfully***, New Delhi: Discovery Publishing House. ISBN 81-7141-678-0.

Ediger, Marlow and Digumarti Bhaskara Rao (2003), ***School Curriculum and Administration***, New Delhi: Discovery Publishing House. ISBN 81-7141-709-4.

Ediger, Marlow and Digumarti Bhaskara Rao (2003), ***Teaching Mathematics in Elementary Schools***, New Delhi: Discovery Publishing House. ISBN 81-7141-687-X.

Ediger, Marlow and Digumarti Bhaskara Rao (2003), ***Teaching Science in Elementary Schools***, New Delhi: Discovery Publishing House. ISBN 81-7141-698-5.

Ediger, Marlow and Digumarti Bhaskara Rao (2003), ***School Curriculum and Administration***, New Delhi: Discovery Publishing House. ISBN 81-7141-709-4.

Ediger, Marlow and Digumarti Bhaskara Rao (2003), ***Elementary Curriculum Improvement***, New Delhi: Discovery Publishing House. ISBN 81-7141-740-X.

Ediger, Marlow and Digumarti Bhaskara Rao (2004), ***Modern Elementary School***, New Delhi: Discovery Publishing House.

Ediger, Marlow and Digumarti Bhaskara Rao (2004), ***School Organisation***, New Delhi: Discovery Publishing House. ISBN 81-7141-843-0.

Ediger, Marlow and Digumarti Bhaskara Rao (2004), ***Relevancy in Elementary Curriculum***, New Delhi: Discovery Publishing House. ISBN 81-7141-845-9.

Ediger, Marlow and Digumarti Bhaskara Rao (2005), ***Quality School Education***, New Delhi: Discovery Publishing House. ISBN 81-8356-022-9.

Ediger, Marlow and Digumarti Bhaskara Rao (2006), ***Successful School Education***, New Delhi: Discovery Publishing House. ISBN 81-8356-054-7.

Ediger, Marlow and Digumarti Bhaskara Rao (2006), ***Successful School Administration***, New Delhi: Discovery Publishing House. ISBN 81-8356-046-6.

Ediger, Marlow and Digumarti Bhaskara Rao (2006), ***Issues in School Curriculum***, New Delhi: Discovery Publishing House. ISBN 81-8356-052-0.

Ediger, Marlow and Digumarti Bhaskara Rao (2006), ***Community College–Curriculum and Teaching***, New Delhi: Discovery Publishing House. ISBN 81-8356-053-9.

Ediger, Marlow and Digumarti Bhaskara Rao (2006), ***Administration of Schools***, New Delhi: Discovery Publishing House.

Ediger, Marlow and Digumarti Bhaskara Rao (2006), ***Reading Curriculum and Instruction***, New Delhi: Discovery Publishing House.

Ediger, Marlow and Digumarti Bhaskara Rao (2006), ***Curriculum Organisation***, New Delhi: Discovery Publishing House. ISBN 81-8356-205-1.

Ediger, Marlow and Digumarti Bhaskara Rao (2006), ***Curriculum of School Subjects***, New Delhi: Discovery Publishing House. ISBN 81-8356-207-8.

Ediger, Marlow, B.S.V. Dutt and Digumarti Bhaskara Rao (2003), ***Teaching English Successfully***, New Delhi: Discovery Publishing House. ISBN 81-7141-707-8.

Elizabeth, M.E.S., Author and Digumarti Bhaskara Rao, Editor (2004), ***Methods of Teaching English***, New Delhi: Discovery Publishing House. ISBN 81-7141-809-0.

Elizabeth, M.E.S., Author and Digumarti Bhaskara Rao, Editor (2004), ***Acquisition of English Vocabulary***, New Delhi: Discovery Publishing House. ISBN 81-8356-075-X.

Fatima, Sk. Author and Digumarti Bhaskara Rao, Editor (2007), ***Reasoning Ability of School Students***, New Delhi: Discovery Publishing House. ISBN 81-8356-330-9.

Gopala Krishna, M., Author and Digumarti Bhaskara Rao, Editor (2007), ***Techniques of Teaching Physical Education***, New Delhi: Sonali Publications. ISBN 81-8411-044-8.

Gopala Krishna, M., Author and Digumarti Bhaskara Rao, Editor (2007), ***Techniques of Teaching Education***, New Delhi: Sonali Publications. ISBN 81-8411-062-6.

Harshitha, Digumarthi, Author and Digumarti Bhaskara Rao, Editor (2004), ***Methods of Teaching Information Technology***, New Delhi: Discovery Publishing House. ISBN 81-7141-805-8.

Harshitha, Digumarthi, Author and Digumarti Bhaskara Rao, Editor (2007), ***Techniques of Teaching Computer Science***, New Delhi: Sonali Publications. ISBN 81-8411-036-7.

Indira Devi, Author and J. Prasanth Kumar and Digumarti Bhaskara Rao, Editors (2004), ***Values in Language Text Books***, New Delhi: Discovery Publishing House. ISBN 81-7141-833-3.

Jalaja Kumari, C., Author and Digumarti Bhaskara Rao, Editor (2004), ***Methods of Teaching Educational Technology***, New Delhi: Discovery Publishing House. ISBN 81-7141-810-4.

Jalaja Kumari, C., Author and Digumarti Bhaskara Rao, Editor (2007), ***Job Satisfaction of Teachers***, New Delhi: Discovery Publishing House. ISBN 81-8356-329-5.

Janardhan Reddy, B., Author and Digumarti Bhaskara Rao, Editor (2006), ***Techniques of Teaching Sociology***, New Delhi: Sonali Publications. ISBN 81-8411-042-1.

Jayasree, K., Author and Digumarti Bhaskara Rao, Editor (1999), ***Correlates of Socialisation***, New Delhi: Discovery Publishing House. ISBN 81-7141-517-2.

Jayasree, K., Author and Digumarti Bhaskara Rao, Editor (2004). ***Methods of Teaching Science***, New Delhi: Discovery Publishing House. ISBN 81-7141-801-5.

John Babu, C., Author and T.J.R. Prasad, G.M. Madhukar and Digumarti Bhaskara Rao, Editors (1996), ***Problem Solving in Mathematics***, New Delhi: APH Publishing Corporation. ISBN 81-7648-273-0.

Joseph Raju, B and G.A. Anitha, Authors and Digumarti Bhaskara Rao, Editor (2004), ***Population Education***, New Delhi: Sonali Publications. ISBN 81-88836-31-3.

Lalitha, T., Author and K.S. Prabhakaram, D.S.N. Sastry and Digumarti Bhaskara Rao, Editors (2004), ***Educational Philosophic Beliefs***. New Delhi: Discovery Publishing House. ISBN 81-7141-765-5.

Krishna, G., Author and Digumarti Bhaskara Rao, Editor (2006). ***Techniques of Teaching Physical Education***, New Delhi: Sonali Publications. ISBN 81-8411-044-8.

Kumar Raja, g., Author and Digumarti Bhaskara Rao, Editor (2007), ***Principles of Primary School***, New Delhi: Sonali Publications. ISBN 81-8411-054-5.

Lakshmi Kumari, V., Author and Digumarti Bhaskara Rao, Editor (2006), ***Techniques of Teaching Home Science***, New Delhi: Sonali Publications. ISBN 81-8411-048-0.

Madhava, K., Author and Digumarti Bhaskara Rao, Editor (2008), ***Personality of Adolescent Students***, New Delhi: Discovery Publishing House.

Madhu Bala, Jampala, Author and Digumarti Bhaskara Rao, Editor (2004), ***Methods of Teaching Exceptional Children***, New Delhi: Discovery Publishing House. ISBN 81-7141-802-3.

Madhu Bala, Jampala, Author and Digumarti Bhaskara Rao, Editor (2007), ***Adjustment, Problems of Hearing Impaired,*** New Delhi: Discovery Publishing House. ISBN 81-7141-831-7.

Marja, Talvi and Digumarti Bhaskara Rao, Editors (1996), ***Educational Leadership and Social Changes,*** New Delhi: Discovery Publishing House. ISBN 81-7141-320-X.

Nageswara Rao, S. and M. Srihari, Authors and Digumarti Bhaskara Rao, Editor (2004), ***Guidance and Counselling,*** New Delhi: Discovery Publishing House. ISBN 81-7141-840-6.

Nageswara Rao, S., Author and Digumarti Bhaskara Rao, Editor (2006), ***Techniques of Teaching Psychology,*** New Delhi: Sonali Publications. ISBN 81-8411-040-5.

Nageswara Rao, S. and P. Sridhar, Authors and Digumarti Bhaskara Rao, Editor (2004), ***Methods and Techniques of Teaching,*** New Delhi: Sonali Publications. ISBN 81-88836-33-8.

Nirmala Jyothi, M., Author and Digumarti Bhaskara Rao, Editor (2003), ***Non-detention System in School Education,*** New Delhi: Discovery Publishing House. ISBN 81-7141-654-3.

Padma Tulasi, G., Author and Digumarti Bhaskara Rao, Editor (2004), ***Methods of Teaching Elementary Science,*** New Delhi: Discovery Publishing House. ISBN 81-7141-871-6.

Pitchi Reddy, M., Author and Digumarti Bhaskara Rao, Editor (2007), ***Techniques of Teaching Social Sciences,*** New Delhi: Sonali Publications. ISBN 81-8411-066-X.

Prasad Babu, B., Author and P. Madhu and Digumarti Bhaskara Rao, Editors (2006), ***Psychological Adjustment and Well-being,*** New Delhi: Discovery Publishing House. ISBN 81-8356-204-3.

Prasad Babu, B., Author and M.V.R. Raju and Digumarti Bhaskara Rao, Editors (2006), ***Behavioural Problems of School Children,*** New Delhi: Discovery Publishing House. ISBN 81-8356-206-X.

Prasada Rao, V.P., Author and K.N. Rani and D. Bhaskara Rao, Editors (2004), ***India Pakistan: Partition Perspectives in Indo English Novels,*** New Delhi: Discovery Publishing House. ISBN 81-7141-871-6.

Prabhakaram, K.S., Author and Digumarti Bhaskara Rao, Editors (1998), ***Concept Attainment Model in Mathematics Teaching,*** New Delhi: Discovery Publishing House. ISBN 81-7141-424-9.

Prasanth Kumar, J., Author and Digumarti Bhaskara Rao, Editor (1998), ***Effectiveness of Distance Education System,*** New Delhi: Discovery Publishing House. ISBN 81-7141-437-0.

Prasanth Kumar, J., Author and Digumarti Bhaskara Rao, Editor (2004), ***Methods of Teaching Civics,*** New Delhi: Discovery Publishing House. ISBN 81-7141-806-6.

Prasanth Kumar, J., Author and G. Sundara Rao and Digumarti Bhaskara Rao, Editors (2000), ***Open University Student Support Services,*** New Delhi: Discovery Publishing House. ISBN 81-7141-550-4.

Raja Kumari, M.A. and D.R.S. Sundari, Authors and Digumarti Bhaskara Rao, Editor (2004), ***Special Education,*** New Delhi: Discovery Publishing House. ISBN 81-7141-846-5.

Raja Kumari, M.A. and D.R.S. Sundari, Authors and Digumarti Bhaskara Rao, Editor (2004), ***Methods of Teaching Educational Psychology,*** New Delhi: Discovery Publishing House. ISBN 81-7141-820-1.

Ramatulasamma, K., Author and Digumarti Bhaskara Rao, Editor (2002), ***Job Satisfaction of Teacher Educators,*** New Delhi: Discovery Publishing House. ISBN 81-7141-655-1.

Rama Krishnaiah, D., Author and Digumarti Bhaskara Rao, Editor (1998), ***Job Satisfaction of College Teachers,*** New Delhi: Discovery Publishing House. ISBN 81-7141-438-9.

Rama Kumar Ratnam, M.V., Author and Digumarti Bhaskara Rao, Editor (1998), ***Dukkha: Suffering in Early Buddhism,*** New Delhi: Discovery Publishing House. ISBN 81-7141-653-5.

Rama Krishna Prasad and P. Vide Sagar, Authors and Digumarti Bhaskara Rao, Editor (2004), ***Methods of Teaching Physical Education,*** New Delhi: Discovery Publishing House.

Rama Seshaiah, P. Author and Digumarti Bhaskara Rao, Editor (2004), ***Methods of Teaching Home Science,*** New Delhi: Discovery Publishing House. ISBN 81-7141-916-X.

Rama Swamy, K., Author and Digumarti Bhaskara Rao, Editor (2007), ***Techniques of Teaching Environmental Science***, New Delhi: Sonali Publications. ISBN 81-8411-035-9.

Ramesh, A.R., Author and Digumarti Bhaskara Rao, Editor (2006), ***Techniques of Teaching Commerce***, New Delhi: Sonali Publications. ISBN 81-8411-043-X.

Ramesh, Ghanta and Digumarti Bhaskara Rao, Editors (1998), ***Environmental Education: Problems and Prospects***, New Delhi: Discovery Publishing House. ISBN 81-7141-423-0.

Ranga Rao, B., Author and Digumarti Bhaskara Rao, Editor (2007), ***Techniques of Teaching Economics***, New Delhi: Sonali Publications. ISBN 81-8411-056-1.

Ranga Rao, R., Author and Digumarti Bhaskara Rao, Editor (2004), ***Methods of Teacher Teaching***, New Delhi: Discovery Publishing House. ISBN 81-7141-812-0.

Rani, S.S., Author and Digumarti Bhaskara Rao, Editor (2006), ***Techniques of Teaching Botany***, New Delhi: Sonali Publications. ISBN 81-8411-037-5.

Rathaiah, Lavu and Digumarti Bhaskara Rao, Editors (1996), ***International Innovations in Education***, New Delhi: Discovery Publishing House. ISBN 81-7141-359-5.

Rathaiah, Lavu and Digumarti Bhaskara Rao (1997), ***Achievement Correlates***, New Delhi: Discovery Publishing House. ISBN 81-7141- 385-4.

Ravi Krishna, M., Author and Digumarti Bhaskara Rao, Editor (2004), ***Examination System***, New Delhi: Discovery Publishing House. ISBN 81-7141-824-4.

Ravi Kumar, M., Author and Digumarti Bhaskara Rao, Editor (2004), ***Methods of Teaching Computer Science***, New Delhi: Discovery Publishing House. ISBN 81-7141-823-6.

Rudramamba, B., Author and Digumarti Bhaskara Rao, Editor (2003), ***Problems of Teaching***, New Delhi: APH Publishing Corporation. ISBN 81-7648-462-8.

Rudramamba, B. and V. Lakshmi Kumari, Authors and Digumarti Bhaskara Rao, Editor (2004), ***Methods of Teaching Economics,*** New Delhi: Discovery Publishing House. ISBN 81-7141-900-3.

Sambasiva Rao, P., Author and Digumarti Bhaskara Rao, Editor (2007), ***Techniques of Teaching Psychology,*** New Delhi: Sonali Publications. ISBN 81-8411-040-5.

Sanjeeva Rao, P.C., Author and Digumarti Bhaskara Rao, Editor (1996), ***A Text Book of Geology,*** New Delhi: Discovery Publishing House. ISBN 81-7141-313-7.

Santhanam, T., B. Prasad Babu and S. Sugandhi, Authors and Digumarti Bhaskara Rao, Editor (2008). ***Learning Disabilities and Remedial Programmes,*** New Delhi: Discovery Publishing House.

Santhanam, T., B. Prasad Babu and S. Sugandhi, Authors and Digumarti Bhaskara Rao, Editor (2007), ***Children with Learning Disabilities,*** New Delhi: Sonali Publications. ISBN 81-8411-077-4.

Sarala, M.M.O., Author and Digumarti Bhaskara Rao, Editor (2006), ***Techniques of Teaching English,*** New Delhi: Sonali Publications. ISBN 81-8411-047-2.

Satya Narayana, V., Author and Digumarti Bhaskara Rao, Editor (2001), ***Physical Education, Social Attitudes and Leadership Qualities,*** New Delhi: Discovery Publishing House. ISBN 81-7141-593-8.

Satya Narayana, P.V.V. and G. Krishna, Authors and Digumarti Bhaskara Rao, Editor (2004). ***Curriculum Development and Management,*** New Delhi: Discovery Publishing House. ISBN 81-7141-813-9.

Shamsuddin, Sk. and V. Dayakara Reddy, Authors and Digumarti Bhaskara Rao, Editor (2007), ***Academic Achievement and Values,*** New Delhi: Discovery Publishing House.

Singh, Y.C., Author and Digumarti Bhaskara Rao, Editor (2006), ***Techniques of Teaching Science,*** New Delhi: Sonali Publications. ISBN 81-8411-041-3.

Sirisha Rani, S., Author and Digumarti Bhaskara Rao, Editor (2007), ***Techniques of Teaching Botany***, New Delhi: Sonali Publications. ISBN 81-8411-037-5.

Sivaratnam Reddy, M., Author and Digumarti Bhaskara Rao, Editor (2004), ***Creativity in College Students***, New Delhi: Discovery Publishing House. ISBN 81-7141-697-7.

Siva Lakshmi, G.V. and G.L. Subbaiah, Authors and Digumarti Bhaskara Rao, Editor (2004), ***Methods of Teaching Environmental Science***, New Delhi: Discovery Publishing House. ISBN 81-7141-839-2.

Srinivas, G., Author and Digumarti Bhaskara Rao, Editor (2007), ***Anxiety of Prospective Teachers***, New Delhi: Discovery Publishing House.

Srinivas, M. and I. Prasada Rao, Authors and Digumarti Bhaskara Rao, Editor (2004), ***Methods of Teaching History***, New Delhi: Discovery Publishing House. ISBN 81-7141-803-1.

Srinivas Rao, P., Author and Digumarti Bhaskara Rao, Editor (2007), ***Principles of Secondary School***, New Delhi: Sonali Publications. ISBN 81-8411-058-8.

Srinivasulu Reddy, M. and K.R.S. Sambasiva Rao, Authors and Digumarti Bhaskara Rao, Editor (1999), ***A Text Book of Aquaculture***, New Delhi: Discovery Publishing House. ISBN 81-7141-482-6.

Srinivasa Rao, Mandalapu, Author and Digumarti Bhaskara Rao, Editor (2003), ***Achievement Motivation and Achievement in Mathematics***, New Delhi: Discovery Publishing House. ISBN 81-7141-674-8.

Srihari, M., Author and Digumarti Bhaskara Rao, Editor (2003), ***Values of Prospective Teachers***, New Delhi: Discovery Publishing House. ISBN 81-8356-328-7.

Subba Rao, K., Author and Digumarti Bhaskara Rao, Editor (2007), ***School Education Policy***, New Delhi: Discovery Publishing House. ISBN 81-8356-285-X.

Subba Rao, K., Author and Digumarti Bhaskara Rao, Editor (2007), ***Education Planning***, New Delhi: Sonali Publications. ISBN 81-8411-053-7.

Sudhakar Reddy, Y., Author and Digumarti Bhaskara Rao, Editor (2003). ***Creativity in Adolescents,*** New Delhi: Discovery Publishing House. ISBN 81-7141-659-4.

Sunil Kumar, K. and K. Rama Krishana, Authors and Digumarti Bhaskara Rao, Editor (2004). ***Methods of Teaching Chemistry,*** New Delhi: Discovery Publishing House. ISBN 81-7141-913-5.

Suneetha, G., Author and Digumarti Bhaskara Rao, Editor (2004), ***Environmental Awareness of School Students,*** New Delhi: Discovery Publishing House.

Sunita, E. and R. Sambasiva Rao, Authors and Digumarti Bhaskara Rao, Editor (2004), ***Methods of Teaching Mathematics,*** New Delhi: Discovery Publishing House. ISBN 81-7141-915-1.

Surya Madhava, I., Author and Digumarti Bhaskara Rao, Editor (2006), ***Techniques of Teaching Geography,*** New Delhi: Sonali Publications. ISBN 81-8411-034-0.

Surya Madhava, I., Author and Digumarti Bhaskara Rao, Editor (2007), ***Techniques of Teaching Political Science,*** New Delhi: Sonali Publications. ISBN 81-8411-061-8.

Swamy, K.R., Author and Digumarti Bhaskara Rao, Editor (2006), ***Techniques of Teaching Environmental Science,*** New Delhi: Sonali Publications. ISBN 81-8411-035-9.

Swarna Jyothi, K., Author and Digumarti Bhaskara Rao, Editor (2007), ***Educational Research,*** New Delhi: Sonali Publications. ISBN 81-8411-063-4.

Swarna Latha, C.D., and Digumarti Bhaskara Rao, Editors (2006), ***Encyclopaedia of Biotechnology,*** 5 Volumes. New Delhi: Discovery Publishing House. ISBN 81-8356-168-3. (set).

Swarupa Rani, T. and J.R. Priyadarshini, Authors and Digumarti Bhaskara Rao, Editor (2004), ***Educational Measurement and Evaluation,*** New Delhi: Discovery Publishing House. ISBN 81-7141-859-7.

Vanaja, M., Author and Digumarti Bhaskara Rao, Editor (1999), ***Inquiry Training Model,*** New Delhi: Discovery Publishing House. ISBN 81-7141-515-6.

Vanaja, M., Author and Digumarti Bhaskara Rao, Editor (2004), ***Methods of Teaching Physics***, New Delhi: Discovery Publishing House. ISBN 81-7141-867-8.

Valeri V. Koustiouk, Author and Digumarti Bhaskara Rao, Editor (2002), ***A Text Book of Cryogenics***, New Delhi: Discovery Publishing House. ISBN 81-7141-642-X.

Vamsi Krishna, V., Author and Digumarti Bhaskara Rao, Editor (2004), ***School Psychology***, New Delhi: Discovery Publishing House. ISBN 81-7141-880-5.

Veena Kumari, Balusu, Author and Digumarti Bhaskara Rao, Editor (2004), ***Methods of Teaching Social Studies***, New Delhi: Discovery Publishing House. ISBN 81-7141-899-6.

Veena Kumari, Balusu, Author and Digumarti Bhaskara Rao, Editor (2000), ***Psycho-Social Correlates of Achievement***, New Delhi: Discovery Publishing House. ISBN 81-7141-547-4.

Venkata Rao, B., Author and Digumarti Bhaskara Rao, Editor (2007), ***Techniques of Teaching Chemistry***, New Delhi: Sonali Publications. ISBN 81-8411-057-X.

Venkata Rao, P. and Digumarti Bhaskara Rao (1989), ***A Text Book of Zoology–Junior Intermediate***, Guntur: Vignan Publishers.

Venkata Rao, P. and Digumarti Bhaskara Rao (1989), ***A Text Book of Zoology–Senior Intermediate***, Guntur: Vignan Publishers.

Venkateswara Rao, V., Author and Digumarti Bhaskara Rao, Editor (2004). ***Problems of Education***, New Delhi: Discovery Publishing House. ISBN 81-7141-841-4.

Venkateswara Rao, V., V. Vijaya Lakshmi and V. Vamsi Krishna, Authors and Digumarti Bhaskara Rao, Editor (2004), ***Education For All***, New Delhi: Sonali Publications. ISBN 81-88836-30-3.

Venkateswara Rao, V., V. Vijaya Lakshmi and V. Vamsi Krishna, Authors and Digumarti Bhaskara Rao, Editor (2004), ***Education in India***, New Delhi: Sonali Publications. ISBN 81-88836-858-9.

Venkateswara Reddy, L. and Narayana, M.L., Authors and Digumarti Bhaskara Rao, Editor (2004), ***Education for Dalits***, New Delhi: Discovery Publishing House. ISBN 81-7141-872-4.

Venkateswara Reddy, L. and Narayana, M.L, Authors and Digumarti Bhaskara Rao, Editor (2004), ***Methods of Teaching Rural Sociology***, New Delhi: Discovery Publishing House. ISBN 81-7141-811-2.

Venkateswarlu, K. and S.J. Basha, Authors and Digumarti Bhaskara Rao, Editor (2004), ***Methods of Teaching Commerce***, New Delhi: Discovery Publishing House. ISBN 81-7141-808-2.

Venugopala Rao, K., Author and Digumarti Bhaskara Rao, Editor (2000), ***Teacher Morale in Secondary Schools***, New Delhi: Discovery Publishing House. ISBN 81-7141-551-2.

Venugopala Rao, K., Author and Digumarti Bhaskara Rao, Editor (2007), ***Techniques of Teaching History***, New Delhi: Sonali Publications. ISBN 81-8411-059-6.

Vidya, C., Author and Digumarti Bhaskara Rao, Editor (1996), ***A Text Book of Nutrition***, New Delhi: Discovery Publishing House. ISBN 81-7141-309-9.

Vimala, T.D., B. Prasad Babu and Digumarti Bhaskara Rao, Editors (2007), ***Stress, Coping and Management***, New Delhi: Sonali Publications. ISBN 81-8411-086-3.

Vijaya Bharathi, D., Author and Digumarti Bhaskara Rao, Editor (2000), ***Educational Philosophies of Swami Vivekananda and John Dewey***, New Delhi: APH Publishing House. ISBN 81-7648-309-9.

Vijaya Bharathi, D., Author and Digumarti Bhaskara Rao, Editor (2005), ***Educational Philosophy of John Dewey***, New Delhi: Discovery Publishing House. ISBN 81-8356-024-5.

Vijaya Bharathi, D., Author and Digumarti Bhaskara Rao, Editor (2005), ***Educational Philosophy of Swami Vivekananda***, New Delhi: Discovery Publishing House. ISBN 81-8356-023-7.

Vijaya Lakshmi, D., Author and Digumarti Bhaskara Rao, Editor (2004), ***Basic Education***, New Delhi: Discovery Publishing House. ISBN 81-7141-881-3.

Vijaya Lakshmi, V., Author and Digumarti Bhaskara Rao, Editor (2006), ***Techniques of Teaching Music***, New Delhi: Sonali Publications. ISBN 81-8411-038-3.

Vijaya Kumar, S.J., Author and Digumarti Bhaskara Rao, Editor (2006), *Techniques of Teaching Mathematics*, New Delhi: Sonali Publications. ISBN 81-8411-039-1.

Visalakshi, V., Author and Digumarti Bhaskara Rao, Editor (2006), *Techniques of Teaching Biology*, New Delhi: Sonali Publications. ISBN 81-8411-045-6.

Visalakshi, V., Author and Digumarti Bhaskara Rao, Editor (2007), *Techniques of Teaching Zoology*, New Delhi: Sonali Publications. ISBN 81-8411-055-3.

Bhaskara Rao, Digumarti (1986). **Dhrushya Sravana Bodhanapakaranalu** (Audio Visual Teaching Aids). Guntur: Nagarjuna Publishers.

Bhaskara Rao, Digumarti (1993). **Jeevasashtra Bodhana** (Teaching of Biology). Guntur: Nagarjuna Publishers.

Bhaskara Rao, Digumarti (1995). **Vignanasasthra Bodhana** (Teaching of science) Guntur: Nagarjuna Publishers.

Bhaskara Rao, Digumarti (1997). **Vidya Manovignana Sastram** (Educational Psychology). Guntur: Creative Press.

Bhaskara Rao, Digumarti (1998). **DSC Study Material.** Guntur: Nagarjuna Publishers.

Bhaskara Rao, Digumarti (1998). **Upadhyayudu Vidya.** (Teacher and Education) Guntur: Nagarjuna Publishers.

Bhaskara Rao, Digumarti (1998). **Vidya Drukpadalu** (Perspectives of Education). Guntur: Nagarjuna Publishers.

Bhaskara Rao, Digumarti (1999). **EdCET Teaching Aptitude.** Guntur: Nagarjuna Publishers.

Bhaskara Rao, Digumarti (2001). **Bharata Samajamulo Upadyayudu Vidhya** (Teacher and Education in Emerging Indian Society). Guntur: Sri Nagarjuna Publishers.

Bhaskara Rao, Digumarti (2001). **Bhoutika Sastra Bodhana Padhatulu** (Methods of Teaching Physical Science). Guntur: Sri Nagarjuna Publishers.

Bhaskara Rao, Digumarti (2001). **Jeeva Sastra Bodhana Padhatulu** (Methods of Teaching Biology).Guntur: Sri Nagarjuna Publishers.

Bhaskara Rao, Digumarti (2001). **Vidya Manovignana Sastram** (Educational Psychology). Guntur: Sri Nagarjuna Publishers.

Bhaskara Rao, Digumarti (2003). **Patasala Yajamanyam/ Paripalana** (School Management and Administration). Guntur: Sri Nagarjuna Publishers.

Gopala Krishna, G., A. Rama Krishna, K. Subba Rao and Bhaskara Rao, Digumarti (2004). **Jeevasashtra Bodhana Padhatulu** (Methods of Teaching of Biological science). Guntur: Sri Nagarjuna Publishers.

Krishna Murthy, V., K.S. Sudheer Reddy and Digumarti Bhaskara Rao (2004). **Vidya Manovignana Sastra Adharalu** (Foundations of Educational Psychology). Guntur: Sri Nagarjuna Publishers.

Lalini, V., V. Dayakara Reddy, M. Srihari and Digumarti Bhaskara Rao (2004). **Vidya Adharalu** (Foundations of Education). Guntur: Sri Nagarjuna Publishers.

Subba Rao, K.P., P. Ayodhya and Digumarti Bhaskara Rao (2004). **Patasala Yajamanyam – Vidhya Vyavasthalu** (School Management and Systems of Education). Guntur: Sri Nagarjuna Publishers.

Sudhakar, V., B. Ravindra Babu, D.S. Kumar and Digumarti Bhaskara Rao (2004). **Vidya Sanketika Sastram – Computer Vidhya** (Educational Technology and Computer Education). Guntur: Sri Nagarjuna Publishers.

Index